Date: 12/15/21

641.815 AND
Andersson, Linda M.,
Homemade bread /

PALM BEACH COUNTY
LIBRARY SYSTEM
3650 SUMMIT BLVD.
WEST PALM BEACH, FL 33406

Copyright © 2016 by Semic Press, a division of the Bonnier Group

First published by Bokförlaget Semic, Sundbyberg, Sweden

First Skyhorse Publishing Edition 2018

Copyright: 2016 Linda Andersson
Copyright: 2016 Roger Olsson
Translation Copyright © 2018 by Skyhorse Publishing

All rights reserved. No part of this book may be reproduced in any manner without the express written consent of the publisher, except in the case of brief excerpts in critical reviews or articles. All inquiries should be addressed to Skyhorse Publishing, 307 West 36th Street, 11th Floor, New York, NY 10018.

Skyhorse Publishing books may be purchased in bulk at special discounts for sales promotion, corporate gifts, fund-raising, or educational purposes. Special editions can also be created to specifications. For details, gifts, fund-raising, or educational purposes. Special editions can also be created to specifications. For details, contact the Special Sales Department, Skyhorse Publishing, 307 West 36th Street, 11th Floor, New York, NY 10018 or info@skyhorsepublishing.com.

Skyhorse® and Skyhorse Publishing® are registered trademarks of Skyhorse Publishing, Inc.®, a Delaware corporation.

Visit our website at www.skyhorsepublishing.com.

10 9 8 7 6 5 4 3 2 1

Library of Congress Cataloging-in-Publication Data is available on file.

Photographer: Roger Olsson
Graphic design: Monica Sundberg
Editor: Eva Bergman
Reproduction: TB Produktion

Print ISBN: 978-1-5107-3017-5
E-Book ISBN: 978-1-5107-3022-9

Printed in China

TABLE OF CONTENTS

Foreword	1
Handy Tips and Pointers	2
Sesame Seed Pull-Apart Bread	6
Crunchy Rye Crispbread	9
Thin Graham Crispbread	10
Hönö Flatbreads	12
Quick Kavring (Black Rye Bread)	14
Bread with Fermented Milk and Lingonberries	16
Quick Carrot Flatbread	18
Breakfast Rolls	20
Lingonberry Squares on a Baking Sheet	22
A Simple Loaf of Bread Baked in Papera (En Papillotte)	25
Cracked Rye Loaf	26
Rye Kusar Baked in a Half-Sheet Pan	28
Classic Tea Breads	30
Rye Triangles with Carrots Baked in a Half Sheet Pan	33
Grain-Free Bread with Cottage Cheese and Seeds	35
Homemade Digestive Biscuits	36
Cheese Crescent Rolls	38
"Polar" Rolls—Flat Rolls from the North	41
Four-Minute Skillet Bread	42
Snipped Carrot Rolls	44
Flatbread	46
Wort Loaf	48
Spelt Flour Kusar	50
Fermented Milk Loaf with Apricots and Seeds	52
Oatmeal Rolls	55
Rosemary-Flavored Seed Crispbread	56
Rustic Rye Rounds	58
Toaster Bread	61
Mini Loaves	62
Simple Sifted Rye & Wheat Blend	64
Scones	66
Dutch Oven Bread	68
Crunchy Seed Crispbread	70
Sifted Rye & Wheat Blend	72
Pull-Apart Bread with Seeds	74
Simple Pan-Baked Breakfast Bread	76
Quick Seed Rolls	78
Skillet Bread with Salt Flakes	80
Baguettes	82
Moist Carrot Loaf	84
Striped Pull-Apart Bread with Salt Flakes	86
Dinner Rolls	88
Grissini	90
Garlic Rolls with Salt Flakes	92

Pita Bread	94
Hamburger Buns	97
Hot Dog Buns	98
Salami and Mozzarella-Filled Tortano	100
Pizza Buns	103
Pizza	104
Calzone/Pizza Turnover	107
Troubleshooting	108
Index	110
Additional Notes Regarding Ingredients	111

FOREWORD

I just love watching dough rise. It's easy to combine the necessary ingredients and then let the mix rest and grow, mature and change—just like a living thing. Eventually, when it has been shaped, proofed, and baked, the dough's transformation is complete, and from out of the oven emerges golden, deliciously aromatic bread with a firm crust and a soft, irresistible interior. Or maybe it's crunchy crispbread you'll get to bite into, or soft rye rolls reminiscent of childhood. Personally, I don't think anything beats a slice of freshly baked bread or a crusty roll with a pat of butter melting on top.

I'm a home economics and consumer education teacher as well as a journalist. Since 2009, I've created many recipes for Sweden's largest baking magazine *Hembakat* [*Home Baked*]. For a few years now, my blog, "Linda's Baking School," has been one of Sweden's most popular baking websites. I receive a lot of feedback from readers who like that my recipes are simple, easy to follow, and that I show all the important stages of the process with step-by-step pictures. The end results are also thoroughly tested: my partner and I have five children, so we do put away quite a lot of bread in our home.

In this book, I've collected many of my most beloved bread recipes—breads that I hope will inspire more people to do some baking of their own. It's healthier for you and easier on your wallet, not to mention far, far tastier.

Best of luck!
Linda

Note: Please be sure to consult the "Additional Notes Regarding Ingredients" section at the back of the book.

HANDY TIPS AND POINTERS
to help you achieve bread-baking success

Read the recipe: Always start by reading the recipe all the way through, then gather all the ingredients and utensils that you'll need. Now you're ready to begin baking.

Liquid: When you use water for making bread, the inner crumb will be slightly chewy and have uneven air bubbles; the surface will become crusty and quite pale as it bakes. Using milk in the dough yields a softer crumb with fine air bubbles and a softer crust that browns more quickly. You can also use beer or vegetable juice, both of which deliver fuller flavor and a golden-brown crust.

Gluten: Gluten is vital for baking a light bread with good volume. Wheat flour contains the most gluten, so half the flour in a bread dough should come from wheat. For the bread to develop proper size, you'll need to knead the dough thoroughly, either by hand or in a standing mixer. Kneading produces gluten threads that protect the air bubbles that form during the dough's rise. The bread will be heavy and dense without strong gluten threads.

Flour: Always add flour in small increments towards the end to avoid making the dough too dense. Better a sticky dough than a dry, hard one. The dough should feel pliable and have a slightly sticky surface. Always flour your hands when kneading dough.

Salt: Salt will bind the liquid and make the bread less crumbly. It enhances other flavors and imparts better volume, an even crumb, and deeper color. The amount of salt must be just enough—about 1 ½ to 2 percent of the flour's weight. Too much or too little salt will make the dough too loose; and too much salt impedes the activity of the yeast.

Fats: Adding a pat of butter or a few tablespoons of oil to the dough makes it softer and more elastic. It also helps to bind the air bubbles and makes the rise stronger. Solid fats like butter produce the largest volume breads because solid fat traps more air in the dough. The flavor is enhanced, too, producing a tastier bread. Oil is mostly used in savory breads.

Fiber: You can add more fiber, minerals, and vitamins to the bread by incorporating bran, sprouted grains, or crushed grains. Add 1/4 cup–1/2 cup to a regular-sized dough. You might need a little less wheat flour.

Fermentation/rising: Yeast is a single-celled fungus made of water, protein, fat, carbohydrates, minerals, and vitamin Bs. It is a living culture that grows quickly in the right conditions. The dough becomes porous during the rise because carbon dioxide is created when the starch breaks down. This is what creates the air bubbles you often see in bread. The dough must be given plenty of time to rise and mature if the bread is to have volume and be airy.

First rise: Shape the dough into a ball and put it in a bowl. Dust it with some flour and cover it with a kitchen towel or some plastic wrap—that way you maintain humidity and warmth, so the dough will rise better. Keep the dough in a warm and draft-free location to encourage it to rise. You can also boost the rise by setting the dough bowl inside a bowl of lukewarm water, but the bread's flavors won't bloom as nicely. When the dough has about doubled in size, it is ready. Test by pressing on the dough's surface with your finger—the dough is good to go when it springs back.

Second rise (proofing): Once the dough has been kneaded and shaped, it needs to rise a second time to bring more air into the dough before it's time to bake it. About 30 minutes is long enough, typically, but times can vary. Preheat the oven well in advance so the dough doesn't over-proof, otherwise it could easily collapse and go flat. However, if this should occur, knead the dough again and make some new bread.

Some yeast manufacturers advise against freezing fresh yeast, claiming that the cells might burst and hamper the yeast's rising power. However, private testing has shown that fresh yeast often freezes very well.

Cold rise: In most bread recipes, the dough is supposed to rise at room temperature and we use liquid that is tepid, about 98.6°F, to speed up the rising process. This works well, but you can also use cold liquid and let the dough rise in the refrigerator—what is referred to as a cold rise. It requires much more time to rise, but on the plus side, the gluten threads get stronger, the dough becomes more porous, and the bread develops a deeper flavor. You can often cut the amount of yeast in half, thanks to the prolonged rise. The end-product is equally good with both methods, so whichever one you choose to work with is a matter of personal preference. All savory breads can be made using a cold rise.

Instructions: Make the dough according to the recipes that follow, except use cold liquid. Transfer the dough to a bowl and cover it; let it rise in the refrigerator overnight. In the morning, knead the dough and shape the bread, and let it proof on the baking sheet as directed by the recipe. You can also shape the bread and put it in a baking pan to rise overnight, that way you can bake the bread as soon as you get out of bed.

Dry yeast: Dry yeast works just as well as fresh yeast for baking bread. The differences between the two are that dry yeast can be stored at room temperature, has a longer shelf life, and needs warmer liquid (approx. 113°F) to rise properly. Four teaspoons of dry yeast are equivalent to a 1 ¾ oz packet of fresh yeast.

Baking powder: Baking powder is a chemical leavening product that doesn't require any rising before baking. It contains acid, bicarbonate, and starch (corn or wheat). When the acid and bicarbonate mix in liquid, they create carbon dioxide, a gas that produces air bubbles in the batter or dough, which makes for a lighter texture in the bread.

A bread or cookie dough that calls for baking powder should not be kneaded because the gluten threads become too tough and the dough doesn't rise properly, preventing it from becoming airy and light. Always make dough with baking powder quickly and without any unnecessary kneading or mixing; otherwise, it will be chewy and dense.

Baking powder breads are best when freshly baked. If you wish to freeze them, do it as soon as they have cooled on the baking sheet. They will taste fresh from the oven if you defrost them quickly in the microwave before eating them.

If the bread contains a sour ingredient (fermented milk, fermented cream, or lingonberries, for example), you can substitute baking soda for baking powder, using half as much of it as you would with baking powder.

Sugar in the dough: Adding 1 to 2 tablespoons of granulated sugar to the dough provides extra energy to make the yeast get to work faster. If you add an amount of sugar or syrup equal in weight to the amount of yeast, the entire amount of sweetener will be used up during the rise. The dough will rise just fine without any added sugar, because glucose is produced during the breakdown of starch; however, it will happen faster with a bit of sugar.

Shaping the dough: Knead the dough thoroughly on a floured work surface, taking care not to use so much flour that the bread ends up dry. Shape the bread to the desired size and put it on a baking sheet or in a baking pan lined with parchment paper. Remember to make the bread so it's evenly shaped, because flatter parts might burn or dry out while thicker areas remain doughy inside.

Baking: Savory breads should be baked at as high a temperature as possible to make them airy and light, but you must adjust the heat to their size. Small breads can cope with higher temperatures better than loaves and other larger breads that need to be baked through before the crust burns. If you bake bread at a temperature that's too low, it might take so long to bake through that the edges and the surface of the bread dry out. Coarse breads typically require lower temperatures than lighter breads. You can use a thermometer to make sure that the bread is baked all the way through. Crispbreads are baked on the higher rack of the oven at a high temperature, which is what makes them turn very crisp and crunchy.

Unfortunately, the dials of most oven thermostats are not reliable. The oven can be too cool or too warm, which will affect the end result. It is therefore critical that you get to know your oven and that you not always trust the time given in the recipe. At times, you may have to bake the bread a bit longer or remove it from the oven a little sooner.

Temperature grading differs slightly between new and older oven models. However, it makes no difference to the final product whether your oven says 437°F or 446°F; just use the number that is closest to what is indicated in the recipes. All the recipes in this book use conventional ovens and not convection ovens, unless otherwise specified.

Storage: When you want to freeze bread, do it when it is freshly baked, as this is the best way to preserve its flavor and texture. Always let the bread cool completely before putting it in a plastic freezer bag. A bread with a crisp crust needs to be kept in a paper bag at room temperature to remain crusty.

SESAME SEED PULL-APART BREAD

The seeds sprinkled over this bread make it look good and taste great. Brush the dough first with some oil, water, or whisked egg to make the seeds stick to the dough.

Makes 12–14 pieces

1 oz fresh yeast, or 2 tsp dry yeast
6 ¾ fl oz lukewarm water
2 tbsp canola oil[1]
1 tsp salt
2–2 ½ cup all-purpose wheat flour*

GARNISH:
Olive oil
Sesame seeds

INSTRUCTIONS:

1. Crumble the yeast into a bowl (if using dry yeast, follow the instructions on the packet). Add in the water, canola oil, salt, and the all-purpose wheat flour a little at a time. Work it into an elastic dough and continue kneading it for a few minutes.
2. With a rolling pin, roll the dough out to a thickness of ¼"–⅓" onto a baking sheet lined with parchment paper. Let it proof under a kitchen towel for about 45 minutes. Preheat the oven to 475°F.
3. Make indentations with your index finger all over the bread's surface, spacing them about ¼"–⅓" apart. Brush the surface with olive oil and sprinkle with sesame seeds.
4. Bake the bread on the middle rack of the oven for 9 to 13 minutes, or until it has developed a nice golden color. This bread tastes best fresh out of the oven.

CRUNCHY RYE CRISPBREAD

Great tasting and wholesome rye crisp bread that's ready to enjoy with butter and a slice of cheese.

Makes about 24 crispy rounds

1 oz fresh yeast, or 2 tsp dry yeast
2 cups water
1 ½ tsp salt
2 tsp bread spices[2]
¼ cup canola oil
3 cups coarse rye flour[3]
1 ¾–2 cups all-purpose wheat flour

INSTRUCTIONS:

1. Crumble the yeast into a bowl (if using dry yeast, follow the instructions on the packet). Pour in the water and stir until the yeast has dissolved. Add in the salt, bread spices, canola oil and the coarse rye flour. Mix thoroughly. Add in the all-purpose wheat flour a little at a time and work it into a smooth and elastic dough. Knead the dough for a few minutes. Cover the dough with a kitchen towel and let it rise for about 45 minutes. Preheat the oven to 475°F.
2. Knead the dough on a floured work surface; divide it into 24 pieces. Roll them into smooth balls.
3. With a rolling pin, roll out only two balls to make round, very thin cakes, about 0.07"–0.11" thick. Go over the rounds once more with a specialty rolling pin called a *kruskavel*,[4] which has a knobby surface. Transfer the breads to a baking sheet lined with parchment paper.
4. Bake the two rounds of bread on the middle rack of the oven for about 7 to 9 minutes, or until they are nicely browned. While the bread is baking, roll out the next two balls into thin cakes ready for baking. Repeat this process until all the dough is done. Let the rounds cool, uncovered, on a cooling rack.

THIN GRAHAM CRISPBREAD

Delightfully crunchy crispbread with great fennel and caraway flavors.

Makes about 40 crisp rounds

1 oz fresh yeast, or 2 tsp dry yeast
2 ⅛ cups milk, lukewarm
1 ½ tsp salt
2 tbsp Lyle's Golden Syrup[5]
½ tsp fennel seeds
½ tsp caraway seeds
3 cups graham flour[6]
1 ¾ cup to scant 2 ¼ cup all-purpose wheat flour

INSTRUCTIONS:

1. Crumble the yeast into a bowl (if using dry yeast, follow the instructions on the packet). Add in the milk and stir until the yeast has dissolved. Add in the salt, syrup, fennel seeds, caraway seeds, graham flour, and, finally, all-purpose wheat flour, a little at a time. Work everything into an elastic dough and knead it for several minutes. Cover the dough with a kitchen towel and let it rise for about 50 minutes. Preheat the oven to 475°F.
2. Knead the dough thoroughly on a floured work surface and then divide it into 40 pieces. Roll the pieces into balls.
3. With a rolling pin, roll out thin, flat breads, about 0.08" thick. Use a textured rolling pin (*kruskavel*[7]) for the last roll to make a pretty pattern on the bread. Using a large piping tip or a small shot glass, punch out an approx. 1 ¼" hole at the center of the bread. Prepare four breads for baking, and transfer them to baking sheet lined with parchment paper.
4. Bake the breads on the middle rack of the oven for about 5 to 7 minutes, or until they brown slightly. Let them cool, uncovered, on the baking sheet or on a cooling rack.

HÖNÖ FLATBREADS

Thin Hönö flatbreads are easy to bake at home and much tastier than their store-bought counterparts.

Makes approx. 4 large round flatbreads

1 oz fresh yeast, or 2 tsp dry yeast
1 ¼ cup milk, lukewarm
1 ¾ oz butter, at room temperature
Scant ¼ cup Lyle's Golden Syrup[8]
1 tsp salt
1 ¼ cup sifted rye & wheat flour mix[9]
2–2 ½ cup all-purpose wheat flour

INSTRUCTIONS:

1. Crumble the yeast into a bowl (if using dry yeast, follow the instructions on the packet). Add in the milk and stir until the yeast has dissolved. Add in the butter, syrup, salt, rye and wheat flour mix, and, finally, all-purpose wheat flour, a little at a time. Work everything into a dough and knead it for several minutes. Let the dough rise under a kitchen towel for about 50 minutes.
2. Divide the dough into 4 pieces. With a rolling pin, roll them out into round breads measuring approx. 10 ½" in diameter, each piece of dough on its own piece of parchment paper. Use a textured rolling pin (*kruskavel*[10]) for the last roll across the breads. If you don't have a textured rolling pin, prick the breads' surface all over with a fork. Place each bread on its own baking sheet.
3. Let the breads proof under a kitchen towel for about 20 minutes. Preheat the oven to 475°F.
4. Bake the breads on the middle rack of the oven for 6 to 8 minutes. Keep an eye on them so they get just enough color, because it happens fast when they're ready. Let the breads cool on a cooling rack, covered by a kitchen towel to keep their surface soft.

QUICK *KAVRING*[11] (BLACK RYE BREAD)

A deeply flavored bread that requires no rise. 'Kavring' is a Swedish classic that's popular year-round, but is an especially welcome addition to the table at major holidays such as Christmas, Midsummer, and Easter.

Makes 2 loaves

- 3 ¾ cup fermented milk[12]
- 6 ¾ fl oz Swedish dark syrup[13]
- 2 ⅔ oz butter, melted and cooled
- 1 tbsp bread spices[14], ground
- 1 tbsp salt
- 4 tsp baking soda
- 6 ⅓ cup sifted rye & wheat flour mix[15]

INSTRUCTIONS:

1. Preheat the oven to 350°F. Pour the fermented milk, syrup, and butter into a bowl. Mix the bread spices, salt, baking soda, and rye & wheat flour mix. Add the dry ingredients to the milk mixture. Mix it all to make a sticky dough.
2. Divide the dough between two 1 ½-quart loaf pans lined with parchment paper.
3. Bake the loaves on the lowest rack of the oven for about one hour. Let the loaves cool in the pans. They will keep well for a few days if stored in a plastic bag at room temperature.

BREAD WITH FERMENTED MILK AND LINGONBERRIES

Lingonberry jam imparts a wonderfully sweet and sour flavor to this bread.

Makes 1 loaf

⅚ cup graham flour[16]
2 cups all-purpose wheat flour
1 tsp salt
2 tsp baking soda
3 ⅓ fl oz mixed seeds (your choice)
Scant ¼ cup dark syrup[17]
Scant 1 ¾ cup fermented milk[18]
2 ½–3 ⅓ fl oz lingonberry jam

GARNISH:
1 tbsp mixed seeds (your choice)

INSTRUCTIONS:
1. Preheat the oven to 350°F. Mix all the dry ingredients in a bowl. Add in the syrup and fermented milk. Mix it all together to make a sticky dough. Finally, fold in the lingonberry jam—you don't have to be too thorough here.
2. Transfer the dough to a 1 ½-quart loaf pan lined with parchment paper. Sprinkle it with the mixed seeds.
3. Bake the loaf on the lowest rack of the oven for about 60 minutes. Let it cool in the pan. Roll the loaf up in a kitchen towel and let it sit for a few hours before slicing it.

QUICK CARROT FLATBREAD

Carrot flatbreads made with baking powder don't need to rise. They have a soft crumb with a crunchy crust.

Makes about 10 round flatbreads

1 tbsp baking powder
Scant 1 ¾ cup all-purpose wheat flour
Scant 1 ¾ cup sifted rye & wheat flour mix[19]
1 tsp salt
1 ¾ oz butter
3 ½ oz grated carrots
Scant 1 ¾ cup fermented milk[20]

INSTRUCTIONS:

1. Preheat the oven to 475°F. Mix the baking powder, all-purpose wheat flour, rye and wheat flour mix, and salt in a bowl. Add in the butter and, using your fingertips, work it into the flour mixture. Stir in the carrots and the fermented milk. Work it all into a sticky dough.
2. Roll the dough out onto a floured work surface. Flour the rolling pin generously so it doesn't stick to the dough.
3. Punch out rounds about 4"–4 ¾" in diameter. Prick them with a fork. Put the breads on a baking sheet lined with parchment paper.
4. Bake the breads on the middle rack of the oven for about 10 to 12 minutes. Let them cool on the baking sheet.

BREAKFAST ROLLS

Wonderfully soft and moist breakfast rolls. Sugar is included to make the rise more efficient, and is used up during the rise and proofing.

Makes about 30 rolls

1 oz fresh yeast, or 2 tsp dried yeast
2 ⅛ cup milk, lukewarm
2 tbsp canola oil
2 tsp salt
1 tbsp granulated sugar
Scant 1 ¾ cup sifted rye & wheat flour mix[21]
3–3 ¾ cup all-purpose wheat flour

INSTRUCTIONS:

1. Crumble the yeast into a bowl (if using dry yeast, follow the instructions on the packet). Pour in the milk and stir until the yeast has dissolved. Add in the canola oil, salt, sugar, rye and wheat flour mix, and, finally, the all-purpose wheat flour a little at a time. Work it all into an elastic dough and knead it for a few minutes.
2. Let the dough rise under a kitchen towel for about 50 minutes.
3. Knead the dough on a floured work surface. Divide it into 4 pieces and roll each piece into a long strip. With a sharp knife or a dough cutter, slice each strip into about 8 pieces.
4. Dip the cut sides in wheat flour, then put them on a baking sheet lined with parchment paper. Let them proof under a kitchen towel for about 30 minutes. Preheat the oven to 450°F.
5. Bake the breads on the middle rack of the oven for about 10 to 12 minutes. They should become lightly colored—not too golden—while baking. Let the breads cool on a cooling rack covered with a kitchen towel.

LINGONBERRY SQUARES ON A BAKING SHEET

Lingonberries bring absolute magic to the flavor of this dough!

Makes about 20 squares

- 1 ¾ oz fresh yeast, or 4 tsp dried yeast
- 2 ½ cup milk, lukewarm
- 2 tsp salt
- Scant 1/4 cup canola oil
- 2 ½ fl oz Lyle's Golden Syrup[22]
- 2 ½ cup sifted rye & wheat flour mix[23]
- 3–3 ⅓ cup all-purpose wheat flour
- Approx. 6 ¾ oz lingonberries[24], fresh or frozen

INSTRUCTIONS:

1. Crumble the yeast into a bowl (if using dry yeast, follow the instructions on the packet). Add in the milk and stir until the yeast has dissolved. Add in the salt, canola oil, syrup, rye and wheat flour blend, and then the all-purpose wheat flour a little at a time. Work it all into an elastic dough and knead it for a few minutes.
2. Carefully knead the lingonberries into the dough. Let the dough rise under a kitchen towel for about 1 hour.
3. Knead the dough on a floured work surface. With a rolling pin or your hands, roll or press out the dough to cover a baking sheet lined with parchment paper. Cut the dough into 5"x4" squares.
4. Let the dough proof under a kitchen towel for about 30 minutes. Preheat the oven to 450°F.
5. Bake the bread on the middle rack of the oven for about 23 to 25 minutes. Let it cool on the baking sheet.

TIP! *You can swap 3 ⅓ oz of wheat flour for the same amount of coarse rye flour (rye meal) or graham flour.*

A SIMPLE LOAF OF BREAD BAKED IN PAPERA (EN PAPILLOTTE)

An easy-to-bake bread that only needs to rise once and that keeps its shape in the parchment paper.

Makes 1 loaf

Scant ½ oz fresh yeast, or 1 tsp dried yeast
1 cup milk, lukewarm
1 tsp salt
2 tbsp canola oil
6 ¾ oz sifted rye & wheat flour mix[25]
1 ¼ cup–1 ¾ cup all-purpose wheat flour
1 sheet of parchment paper
4 paper clips

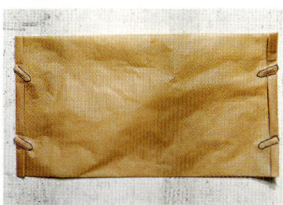

INSTRUCTIONS:

1. Crumble the yeast into a bowl (if using dry yeast, follow the instructions on the packet). Add in the milk, salt, canola oil, rye and wheat flour blend, and then the all-purpose wheat flour a little at a time. Work it all into an elastic dough and knead it for a few minutes.

2. Fold a sheet of parchment paper in half, length-wise. Fold the short edges over and together twice, approx. ½" and fasten each side with two paper clips.

3. Shape the dough into a loaf and roll it in the wheat flour. Place the dough into the parchment parcel, cover with a kitchen towel, and let it rise for about 70 minutes.

4. Preheat the oven to 475°F. Place an ovenproof dish with about ½ cup of water at the bottom of the oven; this lets the dough's surface retain its elasticity during the first few minutes of the baking, which in turn allows the bread to grow bigger in size.

5. Bake the bread on the middle rack of the oven at 475°F for about 10 minutes. Then lower the temperature to 350°F and continue baking the bread for another 20 minutes or so. Let the loaf cool before you slice it.

CRACKED RYE LOAF

A quick, fiber-rich cracked rye bread that requires no rising.

Makes 1 loaf

Scant ½ cup graham flour[26]
Scant ½ cup sifted rye & wheat flour mix[27]
Scant 1 ¾ cup all-purpose wheat flour
½ cup wheat germ
½ cup cracked rye
1 tsp salt
1 ½ tsp baking soda
2 tsp bread spices[28], ground
Scant ½ cup Swedish dark syrup[29]
2 cups fermented milk[30]

GARNISH:
Cracked rye
Wheat germ

INSTRUCTIONS:

1. Preheat the oven to 425°F. Mix all the dry ingredients in a bowl. Add in the syrup and fermented milk, and mix to make a sticky dough.
2. Transfer the dough to an approx. 1 ½-quart loaf pan lined with parchment paper. Sprinkle with some cracked rye and wheat germ.
3. Lower the heat to 350°F as soon as you put the bread in the oven, and bake it on the lowest rack for about 1 hour and 10 minutes. Let the loaf cool wrapped in the parchment paper.

RYE *KUSAR*[31] BAKED IN A HALF-SHEET PAN

Fiber-rich breakfast square rolls made with rye flour and wholesome cracked rye.

Makes about 24 square rolls

1 oz fresh yeast, or 2 tsp dried yeast
Scant 1 ¾ cup milk, lukewarm
2 ½ oz cracked rye
1 ¼ cup sifted rye flour
1 ½ tsp salt
1 ¾ oz butter, at room temperature
2–2 ½ cup all-purpose wheat flour

GARNISH:
Old-fashioned rolled oats

INSTRUCTIONS:

1. Crumble the yeast into a bowl (if using dry yeast, follow the instructions on the packet). Add in the milk and stir until the yeast has dissolved. Add in the cracked rye and the sifted rye flour. Stir the mix, then let it rest for about 10 minutes.
2. Add in the salt, butter, and the all-purpose wheat flour a little at a time. Work everything into an elastic dough and then knead it for a few minutes. Let the dough rise under a kitchen towel for about 50 minutes.
3. Knead the dough on a floured work surface, and break it up into four pieces. Shape each piece into a strip measuring about 11 ¾" long.
4. Place the 4 strips side by side, leaving a space of about ¾" to 1 ⅕" between them. Cut each strip into 6 pieces, cover them with a kitchen towel, and let them proof for about 30 minutes. Preheat the oven to 450°F.
5. Brush the breads with water and sprinkle with some rolled oats.
6. Baked the breads on the middle rack of the oven for about 22 to 25 minutes. Let the breads cool on the half-sheet pan.

CLASSIC TEA BREADS

Wonderfully moist tea breads that are delicious for breakfast with just a pat of butter and some cheese. A true favorite!

Makes about 30 round breads

1 ¾ oz fresh yeast, or 4 tsp dried yeast
2 ½ cup milk, lukewarm
Approx. 2 ¾ oz butter, at room temperature
2 tsp salt
Scant ¼ cup Lyle's Golden Syrup[32]
3 cups sifted rye & wheat flour mix[33]
Approx. 3 cups all-purpose wheat flour

INSTRUCTIONS:

1. Crumble the yeast into a bowl (if using dry yeast, follow the instructions on the packet) and add in the milk; stir until the yeast has dissolved. Add in the butter, salt, syrup, rye and wheat flour blend, and then the all-purpose wheat flour, little by little. Work it all into an elastic dough and knead it for a few minutes. Let the dough rise under a kitchen towel for about 45 minutes.
2. Dust the dough with flour, and using a rolling pin, roll into it a piece about ½" thick.
3. Punch out round breads, approx. 4" in diameter, in the dough with a cookie cutter or the rim of a glass.
4. Put the breads on a baking sheet lined with parchment paper, and prick them all over with a fork. Cover the breads with a kitchen towel and proof them for about 20 to 30 minutes. Preheat the oven to 475°F.
5. Bake the breads on the middle rack of the oven for 7 to 9 minutes. Let them cool on a cooling rack covered with a kitchen towel.

RYE TRIANGLES WITH CARROTS BAKED IN A HALF SHEET PAN

Carrots in the dough make this fiber-rich rye bread moist and flavorful.

Makes about 16 pieces

1 oz fresh yeast, or 2 tsp dry yeast
2 cups milk, lukewarm
Scant ¼ cup canola oil
6 ¾ oz old-fashioned rolled oats
6 ¾ oz coarse rye meal (or sifted rye—your choice)
2 tsp salt
3 ½ oz carrots, grated
3–3 ⅓ cup all-purpose wheat flour

GARNISH:
Approx. 2 tbsp sunflower seeds

INSTRUCTIONS:

1. Crumble the yeast into a bowl (if using dry yeast, follow the instructions on the packet). Add in the milk and stir until the yeast has dissolved. Stir in the rolled oats and rye flour, and let the mixture stand for about 5 minutes. Add in the salt, grated carrots, and then the all-purpose wheat flour a little at a time. Work this into an elastic dough and knead it for a few minutes. Cover the dough with a kitchen towel and let it sit for about 50 minutes.
2. With floured hands, press the dough out into a 9 ¾"x13 ¾" half-sheet pan lined with parchment paper.
3. Split the dough in half lengthwise, then cut it diagonally from the middle to make triangles. Let the breads proof under a kitchen towel for about 30 minutes. Preheat the oven to 450°F.
4. Brush the breads with water and sprinkle with sunflower seeds.
5. Bake the breads on the middle rack of the oven for about 18 to 20 minutes. Let them cool in the baking pan.

GRAIN-FREE BREAD WITH COTTAGE CHEESE AND SEEDS

A grain-free, rustic-style bread that is jam-packed with wholesome seeds.

Makes 2 loaves

5 large eggs[34]
3 ½ oz hazelnuts (filberts)
3 ½ oz almonds
6 ¾ oz flaxseeds
6 ¾ oz sunflower seeds
½ cup pumpkin seeds
5 oz sesame seeds
3 tbsp chia seeds
½ tsp salt
2 tsp baking powder
Approx. 8 ¾ oz cottage cheese

INSTRUCTIONS:

1. Preheat the oven to 350°F. Using a handheld electric mixer, beat the eggs until they're airy and light.
2. Mix all the nuts, seeds, salt, and baking powder in a bowl. Stir this mix with the beaten eggs and the cottage cheese.
3. Transfer the batter to an approx. 1 ½-quart loaf pan lined with parchment paper.
4. Bake the bread on the lowest rack of the oven for about 50 minutes. Let it cool in the pan.

HOMEMADE DIGESTIVE BISCUITS

Tender biscuits that taste amazingly like the originals. They're delicious served with rich cream cheese, or a pat of butter and a slice of cheese.

Makes about 16 biscuits

- 6 ¾ oz old-fashioned rolled oats
- ½ cup graham flour[35]
- ½ cup all-purpose wheat flour
- 2 tbsp granulated cane sugar
- ¾ tsp baking soda
- ½ tsp salt
- Approx. 2 ¾ oz butter, at room temperature
- 2 tbsp milk

INSTRUCTIONS:

1. Preheat the oven to 350°F. Grind the rolled oats to the consistency of flour in a food processor and stir them together with the graham flour, all-purpose wheat flour, cane sugar, baking soda, and salt. With your fingertips, pinch together the dry ingredients with the butter to make crumbs.
2. Add in the milk and work it all into a dough.
3. With a rolling pin, roll out the dough on a floured work surface into a $\frac{1}{12}$"–$\frac{1}{8}$" layer. Punch out rounds about 3" in diameter.
4. Put the biscuits on a baking sheet lined with parchment paper and prick them with a fork.
5. Bake the biscuits on the middle rack of the oven for 12 to 14 minutes. Turn off the heat and leave the biscuits in the oven's residual heat to dry for about 30 minutes.

CHEESE CRESCENT ROLLS

Pretty cheese-filled crescent rolls made with rolled-up triangles of dough.

Makes about 16 crescent rolls

1 oz fresh yeast, or 2 tsp dried yeast
1 ¼ cup milk, lukewarm
1 tsp salt
¾ oz butter, at room temperature
3–3 ½ cup all-purpose wheat flour

FILLING:
Approx. 3 ½ oz cheese (your choice; Havarti, shredded Muenster, and Gruyere all will work well), grated*

GARNISH:
1 large egg[36]
Sesame seeds

INSTRUCTIONS:

1. Crumble the yeast into a bowl (if using dry yeast, follow the instructions on the packet), and add in the milk; stir until the yeast has dissolved. Add in the salt, butter, and then the all-purpose wheat flour a little at a time. Work it all into an elastic dough and knead it for a few minutes. Cover the dough with a kitchen towel and let it rise for about 45 minutes.
2. Divide the dough into two pieces. Using a rolling pin, roll the pieces into rounds, approx. ¼" thick, on a floured work surface. Divide each round into 8 triangles using a pizza cutter or a sharp knife.
3. Place a small pile of grated cheese on the wide end of the triangle. Roll up the triangle, starting from the wide end and ending at the pointy end. Bend the rolls into crescent shapes, and place them (with the pointy end tucked underneath) on a baking sheet lined with parchment paper. Let the crescent rolls proof for about 30 minutes under a kitchen towel. Preheat the oven to 450°F.
4. Brush the crescent rolls with lightly whisked egg and sprinkle with sesame seeds.
5. Bake the rolls on the middle rack of the oven for about 13 to 15 minutes. Let them cool on a cooling rack.

"POLAR" ROLLS[37] — FLAT ROLLS FROM THE NORTH

Soft, flat, well-loved rolls that are always gone in a flash.

Makes about 14–16 flat rolls

- 1 ¾ oz fresh yeast, or 4 tsp dried yeast
- 1 cup milk, lukewarm
- Approx. 2 ½ oz butter, at room temperature
- 2 ½ fl oz Lyle's Golden Syrup[38]
- 1 ½ tsp salt
- 2 ½ cup sifted rye & wheat flour mix[39]
- 2 ½–3 cups all-purpose wheat flour

INSTRUCTIONS:

1. Crumble the yeast into a bowl (if using dry yeast, follow the instructions on the packet) and add in the milk; stir until the yeast has dissolved. Add in the butter, syrup, salt, rye & wheat flour blend, and then the all-purpose wheat flour bit by bit. Work it into an elastic dough and knead it for a few minutes. Let the dough rise under a kitchen towel for about 50 minutes.
2. With a rolling pin, roll out the dough on a floured work surface until it's about ⅓" thick. Use a rolling pin with a textured surface (the *kruskavel*[40]) for the last roll-over, or prick the breads' surface with a fork.
3. Punch out rounds about 5"–5 ½" in diameter.
4. Put the rounds on a baking sheet lined with parchment paper. Let them proof under a kitchen towel for about 30 minutes. Preheat the oven to 475°F.
5. Bake the breads on the middle rack of the oven for about 8 to 9 minutes. Let them cool on a cooling rack under a kitchen towel.

FOUR-MINUTE SKILLET BREAD

Super quick skillet flatbreads that don't need to rise. They're at their best eaten straight out of the skillet.

Makes 8 round flatbreads

Approx. 2 ¼ oz butter, at room temperature
1 cup all-purpose wheat flour
1 ½ tsp baking powder
1 tsp salt
1 cup fermented milk[41]

INSTRUCTIONS:

1. With your fingertips, press together butter and dry ingredients until they become crumbs. Add in the fermented milk and work the mixture into a dough.
2. Split the dough into 8 pieces.
3. On a floured work surface, roll or press out the pieces into rounds about ¼" thick.
4. Heat a dry cast iron skillet over medium heat (Teflon pans work too, but the breads may take a little longer to cook). Dust some flour in the dry skillet. Fry the breads for about 2 minutes on each side, until they develop browned spots. Adjust the heat so the breads don't burn.

SNIPPED CARROT ROLLS

The carrots in the dough make this bread super soft and flavorful. Each roll gets its unique shape from snipping the dough into pieces. Plus, you don't get sticky dough on your hands.

Makes about 18 rolls

1 oz fresh yeast, or 2 tsp dried yeast
1 ¾ cup milk, lukewarm
1 ½ tsp salt
2 tbsp canola oil
2 ½ oz carrots, grated fine
6 ¾ oz graham flour[42]
3–3 ½ cups all-purpose wheat flour

INSTRUCTIONS:

1. Crumble the yeast into a bowl (if using dry yeast, follow the instructions on the packet). Add in the milk and stir until the yeast has dissolved. Add in the salt, canola oil, carrots, graham flour, and then the all-purpose wheat flour a little at a time. Work it all into an elastic dough and knead it for a few minutes. Cover the dough with a kitchen towel and let it rise for about 50 minutes.
2. Knead the dough thoroughly on a floured work surface and roll it into a long cylinder. Snip the dough with scissors into 18 same-sized pieces.
3. Put the pieces on a baking sheet lined with parchment paper and let them proof covered by a kitchen towel for about 30 minutes. Preheat the oven to 475°F.
4. Bake the breads on the middle rack of the oven for about 9 to 11 minutes. Let them cool on a cooling rack.

FLATBREAD

This soft flatbread is baked in a skillet. It's great for breakfast, but also why not make flatbread wraps with mashed potatoes and sausage or some other tasty filling?

Makes 10–14 flatbreads

1 oz fresh yeast, or 2 tsp dried yeast
scant 1 ¾ cup milk, lukewarm
2 tsp Lyle's Golden Syrup[43]
¼ cup canola oil
1 ½ tsp salt
⅖ tsp hartshorn or baker's ammonia[44]
3 ¾–4 ¼ cup sifted rye & wheat flour mix[45]

INSTRUCTIONS:
1. Crumble the yeast into a bowl (if using dry yeast, follow the instructions on the packet). Pour in the milk and stir until the yeast has dissolved. Add in the syrup, canola oil, salt, baker's ammonia, and the flour a little at a time. Work to make a loose but elastic dough, and knead it for a few minutes. Cover the dough with a kitchen towel, and let it rise for about 45 minutes.
2. Split the dough into 10–14 pieces.
3. On a liberally floured work surface, roll the pieces into balls; then with a rolling pin, roll them into thin rounds, about ⅛"–3⁄16" thick. Use a textured rolling pin for the last roll or prick the rounds with a fork to stop air bubbles forming while the bread is cooking.
4. Fry the breads for about 2 minutes on each side in a dry cast iron skillet. Stack the breads on top of each other and let them cool while wrapped in a kitchen towel so they remain soft.

WORT LOAF

Wonderful aromas waft out of the kitchen when wort loaves are baking. This is truly delicious, flavorful bread! You can make it with or without raisins.

Makes 2 loaves

11 fl oz dark, slightly sweet stout, at room temperature
11 fl oz Swedish Julmust,[46] at room temperature
1 ¾ oz fresh yeast, or 4 tsp dried yeast
3 ½ oz butter, at room temperature
½ tbsp ground ginger
½ tsp ground cloves
½ tbsp ground bitter orange peel
1 tsp ground cardamom
1 ½ tsp salt
Scant ½ cup Swedish dark syrup[47]
4 ¼ cup sifted rye & wheat flour mix[48]
Approx. 2 cup all-purpose wheat flour
5 oz raisins (optional)

INSTRUCTIONS:

1. Pour the stout and the Julmust into a bowl. Crumble in the yeast (if using dry yeast, follow the instructions on the packet) and stir it until it has dissolved.
2. Add in the butter, ginger, cloves, ground bitter orange peel, cardamom, salt, and syrup. Mix thoroughly. Add the rye and wheat flour blend and then the all-purpose wheat flour a little at a time. Mix it all together to make a sticky dough. Cover the dough with a kitchen towel and let it rise for about 45 minutes. Add in the raisins—they can be added to only one loaf or omitted entirely. Split the dough in two pieces and shape them into loaves. Transfer the loaves to two 1 ½-quart loaf pans lined with parchment paper. Dust the loaves with flour and proof them under a kitchen towel for about 30 minutes. Preheat the oven to 350°F. Bake the loaves on the lowest rack in the oven for about 55 to 60 minutes. Let them rest for a few hours before slicing them.

SPELT FLOUR *KUSAR*[49]

Fiber-rich and wholesome small breads are perfect for breakfast or a picnic. Spelt flour is full-bodied and deeply flavored, and contains more protein than regular wheat flour. It requires a lot of kneading—about 10 minutes' worth—for the gluten threads to become solid.

Makes about 20 mini loaves

- 1 oz fresh yeast, or 2 tsp dried yeast
- 2 cups milk, lukewarm
- 1 ½–2 tsp salt
- 2 tbsp canola oil
- ½ cup fiber-enriched rolled oats[50]
- ½ cup wheat bran
- 1 cup graham flour[51]
- ¼ cup flaxseeds
- 3–3 ½ cups spelt flour

INSTRUCTIONS:

1. Crumble the yeast into a bowl (if using dry yeast, follow the instructions on the packet). Add in the milk and stir until the yeast has dissolved. Add in the salt, canola oil, rolled oats, wheat bran, graham flour, and flaxseeds. Let the mixture rest 5 minutes. Add the spelt flour a little at a time and work it all together to make an elastic dough. Knead it for about 7 minutes in a standing mixer, or about 10 minutes by hand.
2. Cover the dough with a kitchen towel and let it rise for about 1 hour.
3. Knead the dough thoroughly on a floured work surface and split it into 20 pieces. Roll them into cylinders measuring about 4 ¾"–5 ½". Transfer them to a baking sheet lined with parchment paper. Slash 4 diagonal slits along the top of each bread.
4. Proof the bread under a kitchen towel for about 30 minutes. Preheat the oven to 475°F.
5. Bake the breads on the middle rack of the oven for about 9 to 12 minutes. Let the breads cool on a cooling rack.

FERMENTED MILK LOAF WITH APRICOTS AND SEEDS

This is an easy-to-bake fermented milk loaf full of healthy seeds and sweet apricots, and the dough comes together in only a few minutes.

Makes 1 loaf

6 ¾ oz graham flour[52]
2 cups all-purpose wheat flour
1 tsp salt
2 tsp baking soda
3 ⅓ oz mixed seeds, your choice
Scant ¼ cup Swedish dark syrup[53]
1 ¾ cup fermented milk[54]
Approx. 3 ½ oz dried apricots, cut into chunks

INSTRUCTIONS:

1. Preheat the oven to 350°F. Mix the graham flour, all-purpose wheat flour, salt, baking soda, and mixed seeds in a bowl. Add in the syrup, fermented milk, and apricots. Mix it all to make a sticky dough.
2. Transfer the dough to an approx. 1 ½-quart loaf pan lined with parchment paper.
3. Bake the loaf on the lowest rack of the oven for about 55 to 60 minutes. Let the loaf cool in the pan. Wrap the loaf in a kitchen towel and let it rest for a few hours before cutting into it.

OATMEAL ROLLS

These rolls are incredibly moist and soft due to the addition of oatmeal in the dough.

Makes 16–20 rolls

6 ¾ oz old-fashioned rolled oats
1 ½ cup water, cold
1 ¾ oz butter—at room temperature
1 oz fresh yeast, or 2 tsp dried yeast
1 ¼ cup milk—lukewarm
1 ½ tsp salt
2 tbsp Lyle's Golden Syrup[55]
3 ½–3 ¾ cup all-purpose wheat flour

GARNISH:
Rolled oats

INSTRUCTIONS:

1. In a saucepan, cook the oats and water to make oatmeal. Add in the butter and let it melt in the oatmeal. Let cool.
2. Crumble the yeast into a bowl (if using dry yeast, follow the instructions on the packet). Add in the milk and stir until the yeast has dissolved. Add in the oatmeal, salt, syrup, and the all-purpose wheat flour a little at a time. Work it all into an elastic dough, and knead it for a few minutes. Let the dough rise under a kitchen towel for about 50 minutes.
3. Divide the dough into 16–20 pieces.
4. Shape the pieces into round rolls, and put them on a baking sheet lined with parchment paper. Flatten them slightly with your hand. Proof the rolls under a kitchen towel for about 30 minutes. Preheat the oven to 450°F.
5. Brush the rolls with water and sprinkle with some rolled oats.
6. Bake the rolls on the middle rack of the oven for about 14 to 15 minutes. Let the rolls cool on a rack covered with a kitchen towel.

ROSEMARY-FLAVORED SEED CRISPBREAD

Crunchy, gluten-free crispbread that is as healthy as it is delicious. You can omit the rosemary if you prefer a more neutral flavor.

Makes 1 baking sheet

¼ cup whole flaxseeds
¼ cup sesame seeds
¼ cup sunflower seeds
¼ cup pumpkin seeds
2 tbsp psyllium husk
⅕–⅖ tsp salt
1 tsp dried rosemary
3 ⅓ oz buckwheat flour (for gluten-free crispbread) or all-purpose wheat flour
¼ cup canola oil
1 cup boiling water
Salt flakes

INSTRUCTIONS:

1. Preheat the oven to 325°F. Combine all the dry ingredients in a bowl and mix thoroughly.
2. Add in the oil and the boiling water. Stir until the dough becomes gel-like.
3. With a rolling pin, roll out the dough between two sheets of parchment paper to a thin dough that covers the entire surface of the parchment paper. Remove the top sheet and sprinkle the dough with some salt flakes. Score the dough into squares with a pizza slicer. Put the bread on a baking sheet.
4. Bake the bread on the middle rack of the oven for about 60–70 minutes. Let the bread cool down on the baking sheet before breaking it into squares.

RUSTIC RYE ROUNDS

Fiber-rich, satisfying rye rounds that will turn breakfast into the best meal of the day.

Makes about 12 round breads

1 oz fresh yeast, or 2 tsp dried yeast
1 ¾ cup lukewarm water
5 oz old-fashioned rolled oats
1 ½ tsp salt
2 tbsp Lyle's Golden Syrup[56]
2 tbsp canola oil
5 oz whole grain rye flour
Approx. 3 cups sifted rye & wheat flour mix[57]

INSTRUCTIONS:

1. Crumble the yeast into a bowl (if using dry yeast, follow the instructions on the packet). Add in the water and stir until the yeast has dissolved. Stir in the rolled oats and let the mixture sit for about 5 minutes.
2. Add in the salt, syrup, canola oil, whole grain rye flour, and the rye and wheat flour blend a little at a time. Work it all into an elastic dough and knead it for a few minutes.
3. Let the dough rise under a kitchen towel for about 50 minutes.
4. Knead the dough thoroughly on a floured work surface. Divide the dough into 12 pieces and, with floured hands, roll them into balls. Flatten the balls into rounds, about ½"–¾" thick. Make a hole in the middle.
5. Place the rounds on a baking sheet lined with parchment paper and prick the surface of the rounds with a fork or a potato tester. Cover the rounds with a kitchen towel and proof them for about 30 minutes. Preheat the oven to 475°F.
6. Bake the breads on the lowest rack of the oven for about 9 to 11 minutes. Let the rounds cool on the baking sheet.

TOASTER BREAD

Enjoy some toast with butter and marmalade. The flavor is almost magical! The small amount of sugar in the dough gets the rising started and is eaten up during the rising process.

Makes 2 loaves

1 oz fresh yeast, or 2 tsp dried yeast
2 ½ cup lukewarm water
2 tbsp granulated sugar
2 tbsp canola oil
2 tsp salt
5 ½–6 cups all-purpose wheat flour

GARNISH:
1 large egg[58]
White or blue poppy seeds

INSTRUCTIONS:
1. Crumble the yeast into a bowl (if using dry yeast, follow the instructions on the packet). Add in the water and stir until the yeast has dissolved. Stir in the sugar, canola oil, salt, and the all-purpose wheat flour a little at a time. Work everything into an elastic dough and knead it for a few minutes; this will strengthen the gluten threads properly, making the bread rise high and become airy.
2. Let the dough rise under a kitchen towel for about 50 minutes.
3. On a floured work surface, divide the dough in two; shape into two smooth loaves, and transfer them to two 1 ½ quart loaf pans lined with parchment paper.
4. Cover the loaves with a kitchen towel, and proof them for about 30 minutes. Preheat the oven to 475°F.
5. Brush the loaves with beaten egg and sprinkle with poppy seeds.
6. Lower the heat to 400°F as you put the loaf pans in the oven. Bake the bread on the lowest rack of the oven for about 30 to 35 minutes. Let the breads cool in the pans.

MINI LOAVES

Everyone gets their own individual loaf. They're great for breakfast, or with a fresh salad, or on the buffet table.

Makes 8 mini loaves

1 oz fresh yeast, or 2 tsp dried yeast
1 ¼ cup (3 dl) milk–lukewarm
1 tsp salt
2 tbsp canola oil
¼ cup Lyle's Golden Syrup[59]
1 ¼ cup sifted rye & wheat flour mix[60]
1 ¾–2 cups all-purpose wheat flour

GARNISH:
Salt flakes

INSTRUCTIONS:

1. Crumble the yeast into a bowl (if using dry yeast, follow the instructions on the packet). Add in the milk and stir until the yeast has dissolved. Add in the salt, canola oil, syrup, rye and wheat flour mix, and the all-purpose wheat flour a little at a time. Work everything into an elastic dough and knead it for a few minutes. Let the dough rise under a kitchen towel for about 45 minutes.
2. Divide the dough into 8 same-sized pieces. Shape them into small loaves and transfer them to greased mini-loaf pans or individual pans. The pans should measure about 3"x2 ⅕"x1 ⅕". (Of course, other types of pans will also work; while the bread may not rise as high, it will still be delicious).
3. Slash a few diagonal slits on the top of the loaves with a sharp knife. Brush the surface with water and sprinkle with some salt flakes.
4. Proof the breads under a kitchen towel for about 30 minutes. Preheat the oven to 475°F.
5. Lower the heat to 425°F as you put the mini loaves into the oven. Bake the breads on the middle rack of the oven for about 15 minutes. Let the breads cool in their pans before removing them.

SIMPLE SIFTED RYE & WHEAT BLEND SQUARES

A rustic, moist bread that is simple to make and that can be rolled out right onto the baking sheet.

Makes 12 squares

1 oz fresh yeast, or 2 tsp dried yeast
1 ¾ cup milk, lukewarm
1 oz butter, at room temperature
1 ½ tsp salt
2 tbsp Lyle's Golden Syrup[61]
3 ¾ cup–4 ¼ cup sifted rye & wheat flour mix[62]

INSTRUCTIONS:
1. Crumble the yeast into a bowl (if using dry yeast, follow the instructions on the packet). Add in the milk and stir until the yeast has dissolved. Add in the butter, salt, syrup, and the rye and wheat flour blend a little at a time. Work it all into an elastic dough and knead it for a few minutes.
2. Let the dough rise under a kitchen towel for about 40 minutes.
3. Press the dough into a rectangle, about ½" thick, onto a baking sheet lined with parchment paper.
4. On the surface of the dough, make a pattern of squares measuring approx. 1 ¼"x1 ½" with a dough scraper or a knife. Sprinkle with some wheat flour and prick the squares with a fork.
5. Proof the dough under a kitchen towel for about 30 minutes. Preheat the oven to 475°F.
6. Bake the bread on the middle rack of the oven for about 13 to 15 minutes. Let it cool on the baking sheet, covered with a kitchen towel.

SCONES

Classic scones are excellent breakfast breads, since they don't need to rise and are quickly put together. They're at their very best right out of the oven and still slightly warm.

Makes 2 round scones

1 tbsp baking powder
1 tsp salt
3 cups all-purpose wheat flour
3 ½ oz butter, at room temperature
1 ¼ cup fermented milk[63]

INSTRUCTIONS:
1. Preheat the oven to 475°F. Mix the baking powder, salt, and flour in a bowl. Add in the butter and with your fingertips pinch together the butter and all-purpose wheat flour to make crumbs. Pour in the fermented milk and mix it all to make a sticky dough.
2. Divide the dough into two parts and, with floured hands, shape two round scones about ¾" thick. Transfer them onto a baking sheet lined with parchment paper.
3. Dust the breads with a bit of flour, and score each cake deeply into 4 parts. Prick the surfaces with a fork.
4. Bake the breads on the middle rack of the oven for about 14 to 16 minutes. Let them cool on the baking sheet.

TIP! *Swap 6 ¾ oz of the wheat flour for graham flour or sifted rye flour if you want a more fiber-rich scone. You can also add ¼ cup of mixed seeds to the dough.*

DUTCH OVEN BREAD

The pot's lid seals in the moisture and ensures that a delicious, crunchy crust forms during baking. Warning: the Dutch oven becomes extremely hot! If it's a cast iron Dutch oven, it will also be very heavy. It is best to keep children and pets out of the way, and to always use oven mitts—keep them within easy reach.

Makes 1 large bread

- 1 oz fresh yeast, or 2 tsp dry yeast
- 1 ¼ cup lukewarm water
- 1 ¼ cup milk, lukewarm
- 2 tsp salt
- 1 oz butter, at room temperature
- 6 ¾ oz graham flour[64]
- 2 ½ cup sifted rye & wheat flour mix[65]
- 2–2 ½ cup all-purpose wheat flour

INSTRUCTIONS:

1. Crumble the yeast into a bowl (if using dry yeast, follow the instructions on the packet). Add in the water and milk, and stir to dissolve the yeast. Add in the salt, butter, graham flour, rye & wheat flour mix, and all-purpose wheat flour a little at a time. Work it all into an elastic dough and knead it for a few minutes.
2. Let the dough rise under a kitchen towel for about 1 hour. Preheat the oven to 475°F.
3. Knead the dough into the shape of a ball, and roll it in the wheat flour. Wrap the dough ball in a floured kitchen towel and proof it for about 30 minutes. Meanwhile, place an empty, 4-quart cast iron Dutch oven (without the lid) in the oven that's heating up.
4. Remove the pot from the oven (Careful! Use oven mitts!) and sprinkle the bottom with flour to prevent the bread from sticking. Tip the floured dough ball into the hot pot. Put the lid on the pot.
5. Bake the bread on the lowest rack of the oven for about 15 minutes. Take the lid off the pot (Careful! Use oven mitts!) and lower the oven's temperature to 400°F and continue baking the bread for another 40 minutes. Let the bread cool in the pot without the lid.

CRUNCHY SEED CRISPBREAD

Crunchy, thin crispbread with healthy, fiber-rich seeds.

Makes 20–25 pieces

- ¼ cup sunflower seeds, unsalted
- ¼ cup sesame seeds
- ¼ cup flaxseeds
- ¼ cup pumpkin seeds, unsalted
- 2 tbsp chia seeds
- 1 ½ tsp psyllium husks
- ⅖ tsp salt
- ¾ cup cornmeal OR all-purpose wheat flour (if using wheat flour, omit the psyllium husk)
- 1 ⅕ cup water
- 2 tbsp canola oil
- Salt flakes

INSTRUCTIONS:

1. Preheat the oven to 325°F. Mix the sunflower seeds, sesame seeds, flaxseeds, pumpkin seeds, chia seeds, psyllium husk, salt, and cornmeal in a bowl.
2. Bring the water to a boil and add in the canola oil. Pour the liquid over the seed blend and mix it all to make a sticky, slightly gel-like dough.
3. With a rolling pin, roll out the dough between two sheets of parchment paper into a rectangle measuring about 11 ¾" x 15 ¾". Remove the top sheet of paper and sprinkle the dough with some salt flakes.
4. Transfer the dough (still on its sheet of parchment paper) to a baking sheet. Even out the edges of the dough if needed.
5. Bake the bread on the middle rack of the oven for about 1 hour. Leave the bread in the residual heat of the oven if it hasn't set in the center. Let the crispbread cool on the baking sheet and break it into pieces when completely cooled.

SIFTED RYE & WHEAT BLEND BREADS

Classic, moist, sifted rye & wheat breads with a hole at the center. Cut them into triangles when serving.

Makes 4 round breads

- 1 ¾ oz fresh yeast, or 4 tsp dried yeast
- 2 ½ cup milk, lukewarm
- 2 tsp salt
- ¼ cup Lyle's Golden Syrup[66]
- 1 ¾ oz butter, at room temperature
- 5 ½–6 cups sifted rye & wheat flour mix[67]

INSTRUCTION:

1. Crumble the yeast into a bowl (if using dry yeast, follow the instructions on the packet). Pour in the milk and stir until the yeast has dissolved. Add in the salt, syrup, butter, and the rye and wheat flour blend a little at a time. Work it all into an elastic dough and knead it for a few minutes.
2. Let the dough rise under a kitchen towel for about 45 minutes.
3. On a floured work surface, knead the dough thoroughly. Split it into 4 pieces and shape them into round balls. With floured hands, press them into flat round breads, about 7"–7 ¾" in diameter. Put them on a baking sheet lined with parchment paper.
4. Punch out a hole about 1 ½" in diameter in the middle of the bread, using a shot glass, for example. Prick the breads with a fork.
5. Proof the breads under a kitchen towel for about 30 minutes. Preheat the oven to 425°F.
6. Bake the breads on the middle rack of the oven for about 15 minutes. Let them cool on a cooling rack covered by a kitchen towel.

PULL-APART BREAD WITH SEEDS

Small, moist, airy rolls sprinkled with three types of seed.

Makes about 24 small rolls

1 oz fresh yeast, or 2 tsp dried yeast
1 ¾ cup lukewarm water
½ tbsp granulated sugar
2 tbsp canola oil
1 tsp salt
3 ¾–4 ¼ cup all-purpose wheat flour

GARNISH:
1 large egg[68]
Sesame seeds
Poppy seeds
Sunflower seeds

INSTRUCTIONS:

1. Crumble the yeast into a bowl (if using dry yeast, follow the instructions on the packet). Add in the water and stir until the yeast has dissolved. Add in the sugar, canola oil, salt, and the all-purpose wheat flour a little at a time. Work it all into an elastic dough and knead it for a few minutes.
2. Let the dough rise under a kitchen towel for about 40 minutes.
3. On a floured work surface, roll the dough out into a strip. Divide it into 3 parts and cut each part into 8 pieces. Shape them into balls.
4. Place the balls in even rows of 6x4, on a baking sheet lined with parchment paper. The balls will fill out and their sides will touch when the dough is proofing. Proof the balls under a kitchen towel for about 30 minutes. Preheat the oven to 475°F.
5. Brush the breads with beaten egg, and sprinkle with sesame seeds, poppy seeds, and sunflower seeds—using alternating seeds for each roll.
6. Bake the breads on the lowest rack of the oven for about 10 to 13 minutes. Let the bread cool on the baking sheet.

> **TIP!** Swap 6 ¾ oz of wheat flour for the same amount coarse rye flour (rye meal) or graham flour for a more fiber-rich bread.

SIMPLE PAN-BAKED BREAKFAST BREAD

This soft, moist bread only rises once, directly in the baking pan.

Makes 6–8 pieces

Scant ½ oz fresh yeast, or 1 tsp dried yeast
1 cup milk, lukewarm
1 tsp salt
1 tbsp canola oil
2–2 ½ cups sifted rye & wheat flour mix[69]

INSTRUCTIONS:
1. Crumble the yeast into a bowl (if using dry yeast, follow the instructions on the packet). Add in the milk and stir until the yeast has dissolved. Add in the salt, oil, and the sifted flour a little at a time.
2. Work it all into an elastic dough, and knead it for several minutes. Shape the dough into a smooth ball.
3. Push the dough into a round, 9 ½" spring-form pan lined with parchment paper. Dust with some flour and prick the dough with a fork.
4. Cover the dough with a kitchen towel and let it rise for about 1 hour. Preheat the oven to 475°F.
5. Lower the heat to 437°F as you put the bread in the oven and bake it on the middle rack of the oven for about 14 to 15 minutes. Lift the bread out of the pan with the paper, and let it cool under a kitchen towel.

TIP! This bread can be cold-proofed. Cover the pan with plastic wrap and let it sit in the refrigerator overnight. Take it out of the refrigerator in the morning before you turn on the oven and let it sit at room temperature until the oven has heated up. Bake according to the instructions above.

QUICK SEED ROLLS

Here are some quick and easy powder rolls filled with wholesome seeds. They have a crisp crust and a soft, moist crumb.

Makes about 12 rolls

1 tbsp baking powder
1 tsp salt
½ cup old-fashioned rolled oats
¼ cup flaxseeds
¼ cup sesame seeds
¼ cup sunflower seeds, unsalted
2 tbsp chia seeds
2 ½ cup all-purpose wheat flour
3 ½ oz butter—at room temperature
1 ¼ cup fermented milk[70]

INSTRUCTIONS:

1. Preheat the oven to 475°F. Mix the baking powder, salt, rolled oats, seeds, and wheat flour in a bowl. Add in the butter, and with your fingertips pinch it together with the all-purpose wheat flour/seed mixture until it forms crumbs. Pour in the fermented milk and work the mixture into a sticky dough.
2. Roll the dough in flour and divide it into approx. 12 pieces. With floured hands, shape them into rolls.
3. Place the rolls on a baking sheet lined with parchment paper and press down on them slightly.
4. Bake the rolls on the middle rack of the oven for about 13 to 15 minutes. Let the breads cool on the baking sheet.

> **TIP!** Seeds are good for you; they're loaded with fiber, which is great for the digestion and the gut. You can go ahead and add a few tablespoons of your choice of seeds to any bread dough without having to modify the original recipe. It works for all bread doughs.

SKILLET BREAD WITH SALT FLAKES

A hearty pull-apart skillet bread. Try serving it with a nice dinner.

Makes about 6 pieces

1 oz fresh yeast, or 2 tsp dried yeast
1 cup lukewarm water
1 tsp salt
1 tbsp canola oil
2 ½–3 cups all-purpose wheat flour

GARNISH:
Salt flakes or seeds

INSTRUCTIONS:

1. Crumble the yeast into a bowl (if using dry yeast, follow the instructions on the packet). Add in the water and stir until the yeast has dissolved. Add in the salt, canola oil, and all-purpose wheat flour, a little at a time. Work it all into an elastic dough and knead it for a few minutes. Let the dough rise under a kitchen towel for about 45 minutes.
2. Knead the dough thoroughly, and shape it into a smooth ball. Press the dough to a round shape in a floured skillet, about 8 ¾"–9 ½" in diameter. A springform pan works well here, too.
3. Divide the dough into 6 pieces with a dough scraper or a knife. Brush the surface with water and sprinkle with salt flakes or seeds. Proof the pieces under a kitchen towel for about 30 minutes. Preheat the oven to 475°F.
4. Bake the bread on the middle rack of the oven for about 14 to 15 minutes. The bread is typically served directly from the skillet.

BAGUETTES

Rustic baguettes with a crispy crust and a light crumb.

Makes about 4 baguettes

- 1 oz fresh yeast, or 2 tsp dried yeast
- 2 cups lukewarm water
- 2 tsp salt
- 2 tbsp canola oil
- 4 ¼–8 ½ cups all-purpose wheat flour

INSTRUCTIONS:

1. Crumble the yeast into a bowl (if using dry yeast, follow the instructions on the packet). Add in the water and stir until the yeast has dissolved. Add in the salt, canola oil, and the all-purpose wheat flour a little at a time. Work it all together into an elastic dough and knead it for 5 minutes in a standing mixer, or 8 to 10 minutes by hand to properly develop the gluten threads.
2. Let the dough rise under a kitchen towel for about 1 to 1 ½ hours.
3. Divide the dough into 4 pieces. On a floured work surface, roll the pieces into 1'–1 ⅕' long baguettes. Place them in a baguette pan or on a baking sheet lined with parchment paper.
4. Dust the breads with some flour and make a few diagonal slits along the top of the bread with a sharp knife.
5. Proof the breads under a kitchen towel for about 30 minutes. Preheat the oven to 475°F.
6. Bake the baguettes on the middle rack of the oven for about 15 to 18 minutes. Let them cool uncovered to keep their crust crispy and store the breads in a paper bag. If you put the breads in a plastic bag, the crust will go soft.

MOIST CARROT LOAF

The carrots in the dough make the breads just that little extra moist and flavorful.

Makes 2 loaves

1 oz fresh yeast, or 2 tsp dried yeast
2 cups milk – lukewarm
2 tbsp canola oil
¼ cup Lyle's Golden Syrup[71]
4 ½ oz carrots, grated
6 ¾ oz old-fashioned rolled oats
2 ½ cup all-purpose wheat flour
2–2 ½ cups sifted rye & wheat mix[72]

INSTRUCTIONS:

1. Crumble the yeast into a bowl (if using dry yeast, follow the instructions on the packet). Add in the milk and stir until the yeast has dissolved. Add in the salt, canola oil, syrup, carrots, and rolled oats. Mix thoroughly.
2. Add the all-purpose wheat flour and sifted rye and wheat blend a little at a time. Work it all into an elastic dough, and knead it for a few minutes. Let the dough rise under a kitchen towel for about 45 minutes.
3. Knead the dough thoroughly on a floured work surface, and divide it into 2 pieces; shape them into loaves.
4. Put the breads into two loaf pans, about 1 ½ quart each, lined with parchment paper. Dust the dough with some wheat flour, and make several slashes on the surface of the loaves with a sharp knife.
5. Preheat the oven to 475°F. Proof the loaves under a kitchen towel for about 30 minutes.
6. Place the loaves in the oven and immediately lower the heat to 400°F. Bake the breads on the lowest rack of the oven for about 35 minutes. Let the loaves cool in the pans.

STRIPED PULL-APART BREAD WITH SALT FLAKES

Delicious pull-apart bread with a sprinkle of salt flakes. You can use olive oil in the dough if you'd like a more Mediterranean flavor to the bread.

Makes 1 rectangular baking pan

- 1 oz fresh yeast, or 2 tsp dried yeast
- 1 ¼ cup lukewarm water
- 1 tsp salt
- 2 tbsp canola oil or olive oil
- 3–3 ½ cup all-purpose wheat flour

GARNISH:
Salt flakes

INSTRUCTIONS:

1. Crumble the yeast into a bowl (if using dry yeast, follow the instructions on the packet). Add the water and stir until the yeast has dissolved. Add in the salt, oil, and the all-purpose wheat flour a little at a time. Work it all into an elastic dough, and knead it for a few minutes. Let the dough rise under a kitchen towel for about 45 minutes.
2. Press down on the dough to cover a rectangular 9 ¾"x13 ¾" half-sheet pan lined with parchment paper.
3. Using a dough scraper, divide the dough into ¾"-wide lengths. Proof the dough for about 30 minutes. Preheat the oven to 475°F.
4. Brush the bread with water and sprinkle with salt flakes.
5. Bake the bread on the middle rack of the oven for about 10 to 12 minutes. Let it cool in the baking pan.

DINNER ROLLS

Light, moist, and scrumptious dinner rolls. Serve them, preferably at a dinner party, with a salad or on the buffet table.

Makes about 20 dinner rolls

1 oz fresh yeast, or 2 tsp dried yeast
1 ¾ cup milk
1 ¾ oz butter, room temperature
1 ½ tsp salt
2 tbsp Lyle's Golden Syrup[73]
3 ½–4 ¼ cups all-purpose wheat flour

GARNISH:
Poppy seeds or dusting of wheat flour

INSTRUCTIONS:

1. Crumble the yeast into a bowl (if using dry yeast, follow the instructions on the packet). Add the milk and stir until the yeast has dissolved. Add in the butter, salt, syrup, and the all-purpose wheat flour a little at a time. Work it all into an elastic dough and knead the dough for a few minutes.
2. Let the dough rise under a kitchen towel for about 45 minutes.
3. Divide the dough into about 20 pieces. Roll out each piece to a round, about ⅛". Fold the dough in at 5 or 6 points towards the center, and pinch them down in the middle.
4. Brush the breads with water, and sprinkle with some poppy seeds or wheat flour.
5. Place the breads upside down on a baking sheet lined with parchment paper.
6. Proof the breads under a kitchen towel for about 30 minutes. Preheat the oven to 475°F.
7. Turn the rolls right side up. Bake them on the middle rack of the oven for about 7 to 9 minutes. Let the rolls cool on a cooling rack.

GRISSINI

Serve these lightly salted breadsticks with a drink, on the buffet table, or as snack in front of the TV.

Makes 50–60 breadsticks

1 oz fresh yeast, or 2 tsp dried yeast
1 ¼ cup lukewarm water
1 tbsp canola oil
1 tsp salt
1 tbsp dried Mediterranean oregano[74]
3–3 ½ cups all-purpose wheat flour

GARNISH:
Water
Salt flakes

INSTRUCTIONS:

1. Crumble the yeast into a bowl (if using dry yeast, follow the instructions on the packet). Add the water and stir until the yeast has dissolved. Add in the canola oil, salt, oregano, and the all-purpose wheat flour a little at a time. Work it all into an elastic dough, and knead the dough for a few minutes.
2. Let the dough rise under a kitchen towel for about 40 minutes.
3. Roll out thin tubes, about ½" in diameter and 9 ¾" in length. Transfer them to a baking sheet lined with parchment paper and let them rise under a kitchen towel for about 15 minutes. Preheat the oven to 475°F.
4. Brush the breadsticks with water and sprinkle with some salt flakes.
5. Bake on the middle rack of the oven for about 7 to 9 minutes. Let the breadsticks cool on the baking sheet

GARLIC ROLLS WITH SALT FLAKES

Delicious garlic rolls that are at their best when still warm, fresh out of the oven. Serve them with a holiday dinner, soup, or on the buffet table.

Makes about 30 small rolls

1 oz fresh yeast, or 2 tsp dried yeast
1 ¾ cup lukewarm water
2 tbsp canola oil
1 ½ tsp salt
3 ¾–4 ¼ cups all-purpose wheat flour

GARNISH:
1 ¾ oz butter, melted
2 garlic cloves
Salt flakes
Fresh parsley, chopped fine

INSTRUCTIONS:

1. Crumble the yeast into a bowl (if using dry yeast, follow the instructions on the packet). Add the water and stir until the yeast has dissolved. Add in the canola oil, salt, and the all-purpose wheat flour a little at a time. Work it all into an elastic dough, and knead it for a few minutes. Let the dough rise under a kitchen towel for about 50 minutes.
2. Divide the dough into about 30 pieces. Shape them into round rolls and score a cross across the top. Place the rolls in greased ceramic or paper muffin cups. Place the cups on a baking sheet. You can also put the rolls directly on a baking sheet lined with parchment paper. Proof the rolls under a kitchen towel for about 30 minutes. Preheat the oven to 475°F.
3. In a bowl, stir together the melted butter and the crushed garlic cloves; brush the rolls with this mixture. Sprinkle the rolls with salt flakes and chopped parsley.
4. Bake the rolls on the middle rack of the oven for about 9 to 12 minutes. Serve immediately!

PITA BREAD

Fill the pita breads with, for example, lettuce, tomato, cucumber, onion, chicken, or a tasty filling. Any leftover breads can be frozen.

Makes about 24 pieces

1 ¾ oz fresh yeast,
   or 4 tsp dried yeast
3 ½ cup lukewarm water
1 tbsp canola oil
2 tsp salt
7 ½–8 cups all-purpose wheat flour

INSTRUCTIONS:

1. Crumble the yeast into a bowl (if using dry yeast, follow the instructions on the packet). Add the water and stir until the yeast is dissolved. Add in the canola oil, salt, and the all-purpose wheat flour a little at a time. Work it all into an elastic dough, and knead the dough for a few minutes. Let the dough rise under a kitchen towel for about 30 minutes.
2. On a floured work surface, knead the dough thoroughly. Divide it into about 24 pieces and shape each piece into a small round about ¼" thick. Proof the breads for about 20 minutes on a baking sheet lined with parchment paper. Preheat the oven to 525°F or 475°F if using the convection setting.
3. Turn the breads upside down on the baking sheet, just before putting them in the oven.
4. Bake the breads on the middle rack of the oven for about 5 to 6 minutes, until they puff up with air.
5. Let the breads cool under a kitchen towel, on a cooling rack.

HAMBURGER BUNS

Home-baked buns make hamburgers taste even better. Bake these and freeze them.

Makes 10 buns

1 oz fresh yeast,
   or 2 tsp dried yeast
6 ¾ fl oz lukewarm water
6 ¾ fl oz milk, lukewarm
1 ½ tsp salt
2 tbsp canola oil
3 ½–3 ¾ cups all-purpose wheat flour

GARNISH:
1 large egg[75]
Sesame seeds

INSTRUCTIONS:
1. Crumble the yeast into a bowl (if using dry yeast, follow the instructions on the packet). Add the water and milk and stir until the yeast has dissolved.
2. Add in the salt, canola oil, and the all-purpose wheat flour a little at a time. Work it all into an elastic dough and knead the dough for a few minutes. Let the dough rise covered by a kitchen towel, for about 50 minutes.
3. With floured hands, make 16 round buns from the dough. Place them on a baking sheet lined with parchment paper, and flatten the buns until they are about ⅓"–½" thick.
4. Proof the buns under a kitchen towel for about 30 minutes. Preheat the oven to 475°F.
5. Brush the buns with beaten egg and sprinkle with sesame seeds.
6. Bake the buns on the middle rack of the oven for about 9 to 12 minutes. Let them cool under a kitchen towel on a cooling rack.

TIP! If you want more fiber in your bread, replace ½–1 cup of the wheat flour with the same amount of graham flour.

HOT DOG BUNS

Easy graham-flour hot dog buns that are great for freezing. They taste much better and are cheaper than store-bought buns.

Makes 20 hot dog buns

1 oz fresh yeast, or 1 tsp dried yeast
1 ¼ cup milk—lukewarm
scant ½ cup lukewarm water
1 tsp salt
2 tbsp canola oil
½ cup graham flour[76]
3 ½–3 ¾ cup all-purpose wheat flour

INSTRUCTIONS:

1. Crumble the yeast into a bowl (if using dry yeast, follow the instructions on the packet). Add the milk and water and stir until the yeast is dissolved. Add in the salt, canola oil, graham flour, and the all-purpose wheat flour a little at a time. Work it all together into an elastic dough and knead the dough for a few minutes. Let the dough rise, covered by a kitchen towel, for about 45 minutes.
2. Divide the dough into 20 pieces.
3. On a floured work surface, roll the pieces into approx. 4 ¾" strips. Place the strips far apart on a baking sheet lined with parchment paper. Proof the breads under a kitchen towel for about 30 minutes. Preheat the oven to 475°F.
4. Bake the hot dog buns on the middle rack of the oven for about 10 to 12 minutes. Let the buns cool on a cooling rack.

SALAMI AND MOZZARELLA-FILLED TORTANO

A sumptuous and satisfying bread stuffed with salami, mozzarella cheese, and basil. Just cut off the desired amount. Delicious for a weekend dinner, on the buffet table, or at a picnic! You can vary the filling to your own liking.

Makes 2 lengths

1 oz fresh yeast, or 2 tsp dried yeast
1 ¾ cup lukewarm water
2 tbsp canola oil
1 ½ tsp salt
4 ¼–4 ¾ cups all-purpose wheat flour

FILLING:
Approx. 7 oz smoked salami, sliced
Approx. 14 oz mozzarella cheese, in chunks
Fresh basil

GARNISH:
1 large egg[77]
Salt flakes

INSTRUCTIONS:

1. Crumble the yeast into a bowl (if using dry yeast, follow the instructions on the packet). Add the water and stir until the yeast has dissolved. Add in the canola oil, salt, and the all-purpose wheat flour a little at a time. Work it all into an elastic dough and knead it for a few minutes.
2. Let the dough rise, covered by a kitchen towel, for about 45 minutes.
3. Divide the dough into two pieces. With a rolling pin, roll one piece of dough into a rectangle about ⅕"–¼" thick onto a sheet of parchment paper. Wrap the other piece in a floured kitchen towel and put it in the refrigerator.
4. Put half of the salami slices, mozzarella chunks, and basil down the center of the rectangle.
5. Fold the right side of the dough up over the filling. Cut the left side into ¾" wide strips. Fold the strips over the dough and fasten them underneath the dough.
6. Place the parchment paper, with the roll on it, onto a baking sheet. Proof the roll, covered by a kitchen towel, for about 30 minutes.
7. Take the second piece of dough out of the refrigerator and repeat the process. Preheat the oven to 475°F.
8. Brush the dough with lightly beaten egg, and sprinkle with salt flakes. Lower the oven's temperature immediately to 450°F when you put the bread into the oven. Bake it on the middle rack of the oven for about 20 to 25 minutes.

TIP! *Pizza buns are great to bring along to a picnic. You can also bake and freeze them to have on hand for a snack. Make up your own tomato sauce or use one that's store-bought—it's up to you. Both work fine.*

PIZZA BUNS

Makes about 24 buns

1 oz fresh yeast, or 2 tsp dried yeast
1 ¼ cup milk, lukewarm
1 tsp salt
2 tbsp canola oil
3 ½–3 ¾ cups all-purpose wheat flour

FOR THE PIZZA SAUCE:
5 oz finely crushed tomatoes
¼ cup tomato purée
1 tbsp dried Mediterranean oregano

FILLING:
Approx. 7 oz smoked ham, cut into thin slivers
Approx. 10 ½ oz mozzarella cheese, grated
Fresh thyme or Mediterranean oregano (optional)

INSTRUCTIONS:
1. Crumble the yeast into a bowl (if using dry yeast, follow the instructions on the packet). Add the milk and stir until the yeast has dissolved. Add in the salt, canola oil, and the all-purpose wheat flour a little at a time. Work it all into an elastic dough and knead the dough for a few minutes. Let it rise, covered by a kitchen towel, for about 30 minutes.
2. Divide the dough into 2 pieces. With a rolling pin, roll each piece into a rectangle about ⅕"–¼" thick.
3. Pizza sauce: Stir together the crushed tomatoes, tomato purée, and oregano. Spread the sauce over the rectangles of dough.
4. Scatter slivers of ham, grated cheese, and fresh thyme or oregano over the rectangles.
5. Roll up the rectangles from the long side. Cut the rolls into slices about ¾" wide.
6. Place the buns on a baking sheet lined with parchment paper. Sprinkle with fresh thyme or oregano if you wish. Proof the buns for about 20 to 30 minutes. Preheat the oven to 475°F.
7. Bake the buns on the middle rack of the oven for about 8 to 10 minutes. Let the buns cool, covered by a kitchen towel, on a cooling rack.

PIZZA

A delicate pizza, made with a time-tested bread recipe, that is just as delicious as one made at a pizzeria. Remember that the oven's temperature needs to be high to bake the pizza straight through while giving it crispy edges. The recipe for tomato sauce is on p. 107!

Makes 1 large or 2 small pizzas

- ½ oz fresh yeast, or 1 tsp dried yeast
- 1 cup lukewarm water
- 1 tsp salt
- 1 tbsp canola oil
- 2–2 ½ cups all-purpose wheat flour

TOPPING (OR PICK YOUR OWN):

- 2–3 tbsp pizza sauce—store-bought or homemade
- Approx. 10 ½ oz mozzarella cheese, grated
- Approx. 7 oz ham, cut into chunks
- Dried Mediterranean oregano

- 4 slices of pineapple (For Hawaiian pizza)

INSTRUCTIONS:

1. Crumble the yeast into a bowl (if using dry yeast, follow the instructions on the packet). Add the water and stir until yeast is dissolved. Add in the salt, canola oil, and the all-purpose wheat flour a little at a time. Work it all into an elastic dough, and knead the dough for a few minutes. Let the dough rise, covered by a kitchen towel, for 40 minutes.
2. With a rolling pin, roll out the dough into an approx. ⅛"–¼" thick crust on a sheet of parchment paper. (Or divide the dough into 2 pieces and roll them into two smaller crusts.) Leave the edges of the crust slightly thicker than the center.
3. Place the parchment paper, with the crust on it, on a baking sheet. Spread the pizza sauce over the dough.
4. Scatter the ham over the sauce (and the pineapple, if using) and the grated cheese. Proof the pizza without a kitchen towel for about 20 minutes. Preheat oven, with the convection setting on, to 475°F.
5. Bake the pizza on the middle rack of the oven for 11 to 14 minutes (slightly less if you're making the two smaller pizzas).

CALZONE/PIZZA TURNOVER

A pizza turnover filled with tomato sauce, ham, and melted cheese that's incredibly delicious! You can vary the filling to suit your own taste. It's yummy whether you use a meat sauce, salami, or—why not—vegetables only (if you want to make it totally vegetarian).

Makes 2 calzones

½ oz fresh yeast, or 1 tsp dried yeast
1 cup lukewarm water
1 tsp salt
1 tbsp canola oil
2–2 ½ cup all-purpose wheat flour

FILLING:

Approx. 4 tbsp pizza sauce, store-bought or homemade
Approx. 14 oz mozzarella cheese, grated
Approx. 10 ½ oz ham, diced
Mediterranean oregano

GARNISH (OPTIONAL):
Canola oil
Mediterranean oregano

INSTRUCTIONS:

1. Crumble the yeast into a bowl (if using dry yeast, follow the instructions on the packet). Add the water and stir until the yeast has dissolved. Add in the salt, canola oil, and the all-purpose wheat flour a little at a time. Work it all together to an elastic dough, and knead the dough for a few minutes. Let the dough rise, covered with a kitchen towel, for about 40 minutes.
2. Divide the dough into two pieces. On a floured work surface, with a rolling pin, roll out one piece of dough to a circle ⅕"–¼" thick. Transfer it to a baking sheet lined with parchment paper.
3. Spread half of the pizza sauce on half of the round (and not all the way to the edge of the round). Put half of the grated cheese and diced ham on top of the sauce, layering them to mix up the filling. Sprinkle with oregano.
4. Fold the calzone in half by lifting the parchment paper to make the dough fall over the filling. Pinch the edges of the dough together properly so the filling doesn't ooze out. Repeat steps 2 through 4 with the second piece of dough.
5. Proof the calzones, covered by a kitchen towel, for about 20 minutes. Preheat the oven to 475°F.
6. Bake the calzones on the middle rack of the oven for about 10 to 12 minutes.
7. If you wish, brush the calzones with some canola oil and sprinkle them with some oregano.

TROUBLESHOOTING

THE BREAD IS FLAT, DRY, OR DENSE
- The dough was not kneaded enough, so the gluten threads didn't develop properly
- There is too little or too much flour in the dough
- The dough was proofed for too long
- The oven was too cold or too warm
- The baking time was too long

THE DOUGH ISN'T RISING PROPERLY
- Proofing time is too short
- The dough's liquid is too warm or too cold
- Too much flour in the dough
- Too much coarse flour in the dough
- Old yeast
- The room's temperature is too cold

DAMAGED STARCH CAN RUIN BAKING
Sometimes bread turns out flat and disappointing, even when you've followed the recipe to a T. One reason could be that the starch in the flour was damaged during the milling process. Damaged starch absorbs 5 times the amount of water compared to undamaged starch, and loses its viscosity (where the dough gets its doughy texture). Instead, it produces a gluey, dense bread.

Typically, about 5 percent to 9 percent of the starch will be damaged after milling, but if you're unlucky, a much bigger amount could be bad. When the starch absorbs too much water, the flour's protein is unable to create gluten, which is vital to making bread that is moist and light. When the starch is damaged, it decreases the flour's ability to retain water, which makes the bread dry out far quicker.

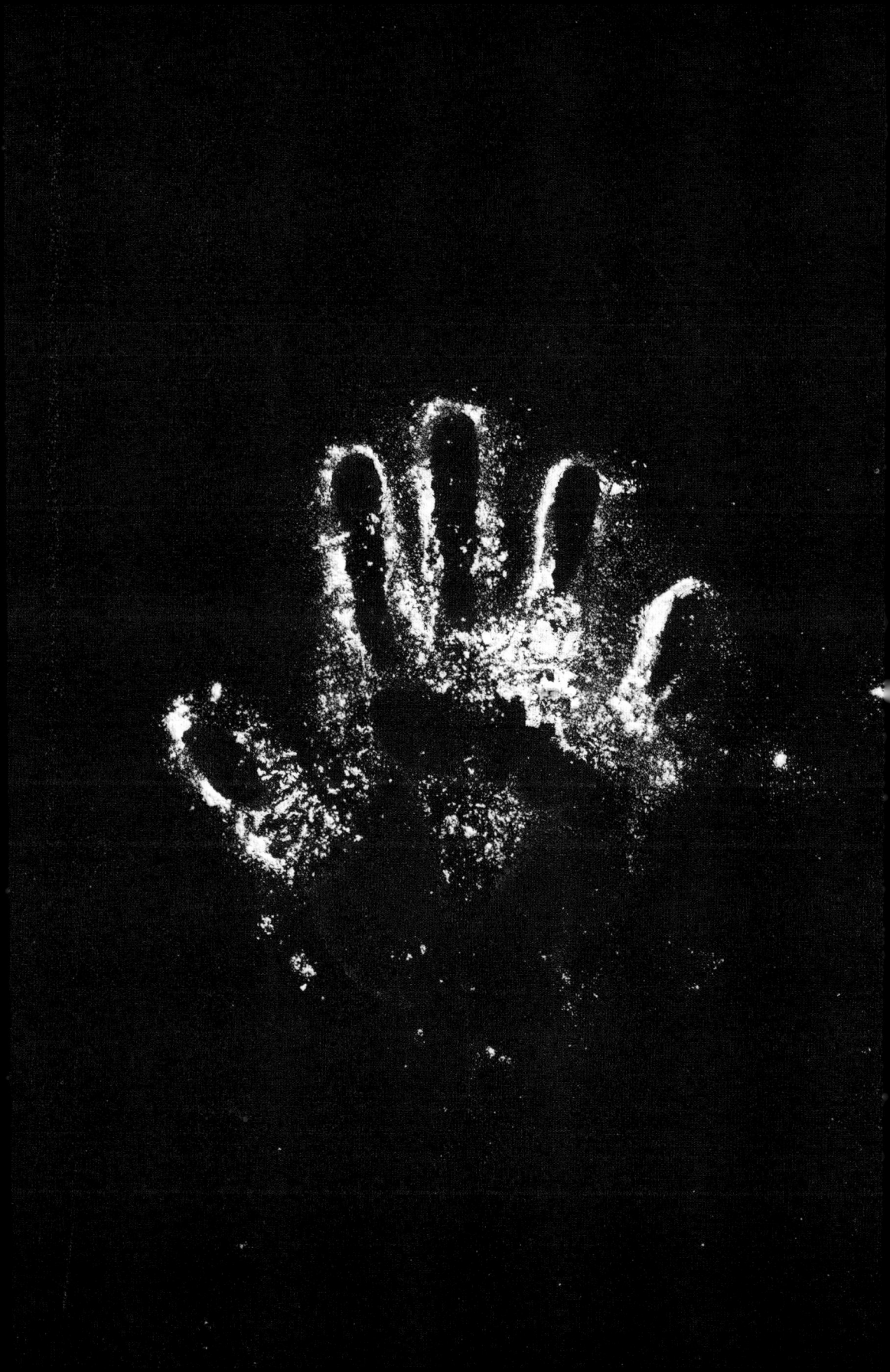

INDEX

A simple loaf baked in paper (en papillote)   25

Baguettes   82

Calzone/Pizza turnover   107
Cheese crescents rolls   38
Classic tea breads   30
Breakfast rolls   20
Cracked rye loaf   26
Crunchy rye crispbread   9
Crunchy seed crispbread   70

Dinner rolls   88
Dutch oven bread   68

Fermented milk loaf with apricots and seeds   52
Flatbread   46
Four-minute skillet bread   42

Garlic rolls with salt flakes   92
Grain-free bread with cottage cheese and seeds   35
Grissini   90

Hamburger buns   97
Homemade digestive biscuits   36
Hot dog buns   98
Hönö flatbreads   12

Lingonberry squares on a baking sheet   22
Bread with fermented milk and lingonberries   16

Mini loaves   62
Moist carrot loaf   84

Pita bread   94
Pizza   104
Pizza buns   103
'Polar 'rolls—flat rolls from the north   41
Pull-apart bread with seeds   78

Quick carrot flatbread   18
Quick *kavring* (dark rye bread)   14
Quick seed rolls   78

Rosemary-flavored seed crispbread   56
Rustic rye rounds   58
Rye *kusar* baked in a half sheet pan   28
Rye triangles with cottage cheese baked in a half sheet pan   33

Salami and mozzarella-filled tortano   100
Scones   66
Sesame seed pull-apart bread   6
Sifted rye & wheat blend breads   72
Simple pan-baked breakfast bread   76
Simple sifted rye & wheat blend squares   64
Skillet bread with salt flakes   80
Snipped carrot rolls   44
Spelt flour kusar   50
Striped pull-apart bread with salt flakes   86

Thin graham crispbread   10
Toaster bread   61

Wort loaf   48

ADDITIONAL NOTES REGARDING INGREDIENTS

1. Author emphasizes unflavored, because flavored and smoked oils are available in Sweden.
2. Swedish bakers use mostly ground anise, fennel, and caraway seeds for savory breads.
3. Whole-rye flour or rye meal.
4. A textured rolling pin used for the last roll-over when rolling out crispbread dough and some specialty breads. It produces a decorative, 'pricked' surface. If you don't have one, just prick the dough with a fork.
5. This is the closest in flavor to Swedish light syrup. It does not taste like American pancake, corn, or maple syrups.
6. This is basically whole wheat flour, but the milling process is different. With graham flour, the various grain components are milled separately.
7. A textured rolling pin used for the last roll-over when rolling out crispbread dough and some specialty breads. It produces a decorative, 'pricked' surface. If you don't have one, just prick the dough with a fork.
8. This is the closest in flavor to Swedish light syrup. It does not taste like American pancake, corn, or maple syrups.
9. Also referred to as "rågsikt" in Sweden. In the UK, this is sold by Swedish manufacturers as "sifted rye flour." This is NOT the same product as the 'sifted rye flour' that is sold in the US. The Swedish product is made up of 62% all-purpose wheat flour and 38% sifted rye flour and malt flavoring. I've called it "sifted rye & wheat flour mix" in the recipes.
10. A textured rolling pin used for the last roll-over when rolling out crispbread dough and some specialty breads. It produces a decorative, 'pricked' surface. If you don't have one, just prick the dough with a fork.
11. Informal term for a kind of dark rye bread made with bicarbonate of soda.
12. Also referred to as "filmjölk" in Sweden. It is a fermented milk available in the Nordic countries. Sigge's and some Whole Foods stores carry plain Nordic-style filmjölk. Buttermilk is close enough in flavor and texture to work as a substitute.
13. Another Swedish specialty item that is, flavor-wise, different from American pancake, corn, and maple syrups. If you only need a very small amount, molasses will do in a pinch. For larger quantities, 1/4 cup and up, use the Swedish syrup because molasses will be too bitter. Swedish online stores and Amazon sell Swedish light and dark syrup.
14. Swedish bakers use mostly ground anise, fennel, and caraway seeds for savory breads.
15. Also referred to as "rågsikt" in Sweden. In the UK, this is sold by Swedish manufacturers as "sifted rye flour." This is NOT the same product as the 'sifted rye flour' that is sold in the US. The Swedish product is made up of 62% all-purpose wheat flour and 38% sifted rye flour and malt flavoring. I've called it "sifted rye & wheat flour mix" in the recipes.
16. This is basically whole wheat flour, but the milling process is different. With graham flour, the various grain components are milled separately.
17. Another Swedish specialty item that is, flavor-wise, different from American pancake, corn and maple syrups. If you only need a very small amount, molasses will do in a

pinch. For larger quantities, 1/4 cup and up, use the Swedish syrup because molasses will be too bitter. Swedish online stores and Amazon sell Swedish light and dark syrup.
18. Also referred to as "filmjölk" in Sweden. It is a fermented milk available in the Nordic countries. Sigge's and some Whole Foods stores carry plain Nordic-style filmjölk. Buttermilk is close enough in flavor and texture to work as a substitute.
19. Also referred to as "rågsikt" in Sweden. In the UK, this is sold by Swedish manufacturers as "sifted rye flour." This is NOT the same product as the 'sifted rye flour' that is sold in the US. The Swedish product is made up of 62% all-purpose wheat flour and 38% sifted rye flour and malt flavoring. I've called it "sifted rye & wheat flour mix" in the recipes.
20. Also referred to as "filmjölk" in Sweden. It is a fermented milk available in the Nordic countries. Sigge's and some Whole Foods stores carry plain Nordic-style filmjölk. Buttermilk is close enough in flavor and texture to work as a substitute.
21. Also referred to as "rågsikt" in Sweden. In the UK, this is sold by Swedish manufacturers as "sifted rye flour." This is NOT the same product as the 'sifted rye flour' that is sold in the US. The Swedish product is made up of 62% all-purpose wheat flour and 38% sifted rye flour and malt flavoring. I've called it "sifted rye & wheat flour mix" in the recipes.
22. This is the closest in flavor to Swedish light syrup. It does not taste like American pancake, corn, or maple syrups.
23. Also referred to as "rågsikt" in Sweden. In the UK, this is sold by Swedish manufacturers as "sifted rye flour." This is NOT the same product as the 'sifted rye flour' that is sold in the US. The Swedish product is made up of 62% all-purpose wheat flour and 38% sifted rye flour and malt flavoring. I've called it "sifted rye & wheat flour mix" in the recipes.
24. If you can't find fresh or frozen lingonberries, use fresh or frozen cranberries
25. Also referred to as "rågsikt" in Sweden. In the UK, this is sold by Swedish manufacturers as "sifted rye flour." This is NOT the same product as the 'sifted rye flour' that is sold in the US. The Swedish product is made up of 62% all-purpose wheat flour and 38% sifted rye flour and malt flavoring. I've called it "sifted rye & wheat flour mix" in the recipes.
26. This is basically whole wheat flour, but the milling process is different. With graham flour, the various grain components are milled separately.
27. Also referred to as "rågsikt" in Sweden. In the UK, this is sold by Swedish manufacturers as "sifted rye flour." This is NOT the same product as the 'sifted rye flour' that is sold in the US. The Swedish product is made up of 62% all-purpose wheat flour and 38% sifted rye flour and malt flavoring. I've called it "sifted rye & wheat flour mix" in the recipes.
28. Swedish bakers use mostly ground anise, fennel, and caraway seeds for savory breads.
29. Another Swedish specialty item that is, flavor-wise, different from American pancake, corn, and maple syrups. If you only need a very small amount, molasses will do in a pinch. For larger quantities, ¼ cup and up, use the Swedish syrup because molasses will be too bitter. Swedish online stores and Amazon sell Swedish light and dark syrup.
30. Also referred to as "filmjölk" in Sweden. It is a fermented milk available in the Nordic countries. Sigge's and some Whole Foods stores carry plain Nordic-style filmjölk. Buttermilk is close enough in flavor and texture to work as a substitute.
31. An informal term for rolls. This might stem from the fact that the rolls often contained oats, as the word is also the colloquial term for "horse" in certain parts of Sweden. *Kuse* (sing.), *Kusar* (plural).

32. This is the closest in flavor to Swedish light syrup. It does not taste like American pancake, corn, or maple syrups.
33. Also referred to as "rågsikt" in Sweden. In the UK, this is sold by Swedish manufacturers as "sifted rye flour." This is NOT the same product as the 'sifted rye flour' that is sold in the US. The Swedish product is made up of 62% all-purpose wheat flour and 38% sifted rye flour and malt flavoring. I've called it "sifted rye & wheat flour mix" in the recipes.
34. Swedish egg sizes run larger than American. An extra-large egg in the United States falls somewhere between a medium and large egg from Europe.
35. This is basically whole wheat flour, but the milling process is different. With graham flour, the various grain components are milled separately.
36. Swedish egg sizes run larger than American. An extra-large egg in the United States falls somewhere between a medium and large egg from Europe.
37. Casual term from the north of Sweden. Polar refers to the arctic region from where the original baker hailed.
38. This is the closest in flavor to Swedish light syrup. It does not taste like American pancake, corn, or maple syrups.
39. Also referred to as "rågsikt" in Sweden. In the UK, this is sold by Swedish manufacturers as "sifted rye flour." This is NOT the same product as the 'sifted rye flour' that is sold in the US. The Swedish product is made up of 62% all-purpose wheat flour and 38% sifted rye flour and malt flavoring. I've called it "sifted rye & wheat flour mix" in the recipes.
40. A textured rolling pin used for the last roll-over when rolling out crispbread dough and some specialty breads. It produces a decorative, 'pricked' surface. If you don't have one, just prick the dough with a fork.
41. Also referred to as "filmjölk" in Sweden. It is a fermented milk available in the Nordic countries. Sigge's and some Whole Foods stores carry plain Nordic-style filmjölk. Buttermilk is close enough in flavor and texture to work as a substitute.
42. This is basically whole wheat flour, but the milling process is different. With graham flour, the various grain components are milled separately.
43. This is the closest in flavor to Swedish light syrup. It does not taste like American pancake, corn, or maple syrups.
44. A raising agent used before the invention of baking powder. Used today mostly for the specific flavor it imparts to certain traditional baked goods.
45. Also referred to as "rågsikt" in Sweden. In the UK, this is sold by Swedish manufacturers as "sifted rye flour." This is NOT the same product as the 'sifted rye flour' that is sold in the US. The Swedish product is made up of 62% all-purpose wheat flour and 38% sifted rye flour and malt flavoring. I've called it "sifted rye & wheat flour mix" in the recipes.
46. A special Christmas and Easter soft drink that is hardly ever drunk at any other time of the year. World Market will sometimes have it available around Christmastime. You can easily make your own: mix ½ cup light beer with 1 ¼ cups of Coca-Cola.
47. Another Swedish specialty item that is, flavor-wise, different from American pancake, corn, and maple syrups. If you only need a very small amount, molasses will do in a pinch. For larger quantities, ¼ cup and up, use the Swedish syrup because molasses will be too bitter. Swedish online stores and Amazon sell Swedish light and dark syrup.
48. Also referred to as "rågsikt" in Sweden. In the UK, this is sold by Swedish manufacturers as "sifted rye flour." This is NOT the same product as the 'sifted rye flour' that is sold in the US. The Swedish product is made up of 62% all-purpose wheat

flour and 38% sifted rye flour and malt flavoring. I've called it "sifted rye & wheat flour mix" in the recipes.
49. An informal term for rolls. This might stem from the fact that the rolls often contained oats, as the word is also the colloquial term for "horse" in certain parts of Sweden. *Kuse* (sing.), *Kusar* (plural).
50. Oats that are 85% oats with 15% wheat bran. Consider adding some wheat bran to old-fashioned rolled oats, if you cannot obtain the enriched oats.
51. This is basically whole wheat flour, but the milling process is different. With graham flour, the various grain components are milled separately.
52. This is basically whole wheat flour, but the milling process is different. With graham flour, the various grain components are milled separately.
53. Another Swedish specialty item that is, flavor-wise, different from American pancake, corn, and maple syrups. If you only need a very small amount, molasses will do in a pinch. For larger quantities, 1/4 cup and up, use the Swedish syrup because molasses will be too bitter. Swedish online stores and Amazon sell Swedish light and dark syrup.
54. Also referred to as "filmjölk" in Sweden. It is a fermented milk available in the Nordic countries. Sigge's and some Whole Foods stores carry plain Nordic-style filmjölk. Buttermilk is close enough in flavor and texture to work as a substitute.
55. This is the closest in flavor to Swedish light syrup. It does not taste like American pancake, corn, or maple syrups.
56. This is the closest in flavor to Swedish light syrup. It does not taste like American pancake, corn, or maple syrups.
57. Also referred to as "rågsikt" in Sweden. In the UK, this is sold by Swedish manufacturers as "sifted rye flour." This is NOT the same product as the 'sifted rye flour' that is sold in the US. The Swedish product is made up of 62% all-purpose wheat flour and 38% sifted rye flour and malt flavoring. I've called it "sifted rye & wheat flour mix" in the recipes.
58. Swedish egg sizes run larger than American. An extra-large egg in the United States falls somewhere between a medium and large egg from Europe.
59. This is the closest in flavor to Swedish light syrup. It does not taste like American pancake, corn, or maple syrups.
60. Also referred to as "rågsikt" in Sweden. In the UK, this is sold by Swedish manufacturers as "sifted rye flour." This is NOT the same product as the 'sifted rye flour' that is sold in the US. The Swedish product is made up of 62% all-purpose wheat flour and 38% sifted rye flour and malt flavoring. I've called it "sifted rye & wheat flour mix" in the recipes.
61. This is the closest in flavor to Swedish light syrup. It does not taste like American pancake, corn, or maple syrups.
62. Also referred to as "rågsikt" in Sweden. In the UK, this is sold by Swedish manufacturers as "sifted rye flour." This is NOT the same product as the 'sifted rye flour' that is sold in the US. The Swedish product is made up of 62% all-purpose wheat flour and 38% sifted rye flour and malt flavoring. I've called it "sifted rye & wheat flour mix" in the recipes.
63. Also referred to as "filmjölk" in Sweden. It is a fermented milk available in the Nordic countries. Sigge's and some Whole Foods stores carry plain Nordic-style filmjölk. Buttermilk is close enough in flavor and texture to work as a substitute.
64. This is basically whole wheat flour, but the milling process is different. With graham flour, the various grain components are milled separately.
65. Also referred to as "rågsikt" in Sweden. In the UK, this is sold by Swedish manufacturers as "sifted rye flour." This is NOT the same product as the 'sifted rye

66. This is the closest in flavor to Swedish light syrup. It does not taste like American pancake, corn, or maple syrups.
67. Also referred to as "rågsikt" in Sweden. In the UK, this is sold by Swedish manufacturers as "sifted rye flour." This is NOT the same product as the 'sifted rye flour' that is sold in the US. The Swedish product is made up of 62% all-purpose wheat flour and 38% sifted rye flour and malt flavoring. I've called it "sifted rye & wheat flour mix" in the recipes.
68. Swedish egg sizes run larger than American. An extra-large egg in the United States falls somewhere between a medium and large egg from Europe.
69. Also referred to as "rågsikt" in Sweden. In the UK, this is sold by Swedish manufacturers as "sifted rye flour." This is NOT the same product as the 'sifted rye flour' that is sold in the US. The Swedish product is made up of 62% all-purpose wheat flour and 38% sifted rye flour and malt flavoring. I've called it "sifted rye & wheat flour mix" in the recipes.
70. Also referred to as "filmjölk" in Sweden. It is a fermented milk available in the Nordic countries. Sigge's and some Whole Foods stores carry plain Nordic-style filmjölk. Buttermilk is close enough in flavor and texture to work as a substitute.
71. This is the closest in flavor to Swedish light syrup. It does not taste like American pancake, corn, or maple syrups.
72. Also referred to as "rågsikt" in Sweden. In the UK, this is sold by Swedish manufacturers as "sifted rye flour." This is NOT the same product as the 'sifted rye flour' that is sold in the US. The Swedish product is made up of 62% all-purpose wheat flour and 38% sifted rye flour and malt flavoring. I've called it "sifted rye & wheat flour mix" in the recipes.
73. This is the closest in flavor to Swedish light syrup. It does not taste like American pancake, corn, or maple syrups.
74. Mexican oregano has a more pungent and citrusy flavor, which isn't ideal for this recipe.
75. Swedish egg sizes run larger than American. An extra-large egg in the United States falls somewhere between a medium and large egg from Europe.
76. This is basically whole wheat flour, but the milling process is different. With graham flour, the various grain components are milled separately.
77. Swedish egg sizes run larger than American. An extra-large egg in the United States falls somewhere between a medium and large egg from Europe.